CONVERSATIONS WITH...
MOZART

CONVERSATIONS WITH...
MOZART

**WOLFGANG AMADEUS MOZART
WITH SIMON PARKE**

WHITE CROW

Conversations with... Wolfgang Amadeus Mozart

White Crow Books is an imprint of
White Crow Productions Ltd
PO Box 1013
Guildford GU1 9EJ

www.whitecrowbooks.com

Text design and eBook production by Essential Works
www.essentialworks.co.uk

Hardback ISBN 978-1-907661-40-2
Paperback ISBN 978-1-907661-38-9
eBook ISBN 978-1-907661-39-6
Audiobook ISBN 978-1-907661-61-7

BIOGRAPHY & AUTOBIOGRAPHY / Composers & Musicians

Distributed in the UK by
Lightning Source Ltd.
Chapter House
Pitfield
Kiln Farm
Milton Keynes MK11 3LW

Distributed in the USA by
Lightning Source Inc.
246 Heil Quaker Boulevard
LaVergne
Tennessee 37086

Contents

Preface

The conversation here is imagined; but Mozart's words are not. All the words included here are his own, taken from his many lively letters and reported conversations.

The only alteration to his original words is the addition of an occasional link word to aid the flow or clarify meaning; and the loss of one or two sub-clauses. But no phrase is altered, and additions are rare, never affecting either mood or meaning.

After all, to discover the man and his meaning is the reason for this adventure. So this is original Mozart; his phrases, expressions, thoughts, and concerns.

Yes, even the evening of wordplay with the Cannabich family; and his less than gallant description of Josepha...

Introduction

Ever since I saw him as a boy of six playing concerts in London, I have wished to speak with Wolfgang Amadeus Mozart. He'd been the talk of Europe then, hawked round the continent on promotional tours by his ambitious father, Leopold. Indeed, I still have a cutting of the advertisement for the London concert that drew me back then in 1764:

To All Lovers of Sciences

The greatest prodigy that Europe, or that even Human Nature has to boast of, is, without Contradiction, the little German boy Wolfgang Mozart; a boy, Eight Years old, who has, and indeed very justly, raised the admiration not only of the greatest Men, but also of the greatest Musicians in Europe. It is hard to say, whether his Execution upon the Harpsichord and his playing and singing at Sight, or his own Caprice, Fancy and Compositions for all Instruments are most astonishing. The Father of this Miracle, being obliged by Desire of several Ladies and Gentlemen to postpone, for a very short Time, his Departure from England, will give an Opportunity to hear this little Composer and his Sister, whose Musical knowledge wants not apology. Performs every day in the Week, from Twelve to Three O'clock in the Great Room, at the Swan and Hoop, Cornhill. Admittance 2 s. 6d. each Person.

The two Children will also play together with four Hands upon the same Harpsichord, and put upon it a Handkerchief, without seeing the Keys.

Child prodigies carry a huge weight of expectation, and some collapse under the weight. So what had happened to the

Wolfgang since? In Germany they had called him 'Wunderkind'; but 'boy wonder' was now a man of 35, and I wanted to hear his story.

Before leaving for Vienna where I heard he now lived, I spoke with the Irish tenor, Michael Kelly, who had stayed with Mozart for a while. I asked him what he was like.

'He was a remarkably small man,' said Michael. 'Very thin and pale, with a profusion of fine fair hair, of which he was rather vain. He gave me a cordial invitation to his house, and I spent a great part of my time there. He always received me with kindness and hospitality. He was remarkably fond of punch, of which beverage I have seen him take copious draughts. He was also fond of billiards, and had an excellent billiard table in his house. Many and many a game have I played with him, but always came off second best. He gave Sunday concerts, at which I was never missing. He was kindhearted and always ready to oblige, but so very particular when he played that, if the slightest noise were made, he immediately left off.'

After a long and uncomfortable carriage journey across Europe, lasting 14 bone-shaking days – and several nights in flea-ridden inns – I finally arrive in Vienna; and like Mr Kelly, find Mozart a most welcoming host. I meet his pets, which include a starling, a canary, a dog, and a horse. One thing I soon learn about Herr Mozart: he does like to be surrounded by activity, which perhaps mirrors his hyperactive mind.

I plan to stay with him for four days, and catch him when I can in his energetic life, as he balances piano lessons, composing, and his Masonic activities. I still regard 35 as the halfway point in life – three score years and ten is the life span the psalmist gives us – so much still to come for Wolfgang. But in the meantime, how has it been so far for the boy prodigy who had to grow up? I look forward to finding out as I sit down for *Conversations with… Wolfgang Amadeus Mozart.*

ONE

Mozart's travels

Mozart is much travelled, both as child prodigy and as an adult, and always for the same reason: to make money. As a child, he was paraded around Europe, with his longest stay in London, where our own King George III was a strong supporter of music, with a particular love for Handel. But though such tours provided brief fame and income, it was always more likely that ultimately, he'd find employment in German-speaking towns. Every country, whether it was Italy, Holland, France, or England, had their own heroes and didn't need another.

And so here we are in Vienna, capital of the Hapsburg Empire, where Wolfgang has lived, in varying degrees of happiness, since 1781.

SP: Well, it's very kind of you to talk with me, Herr Mozart, and I hope you are in good health?

WAM: You may hope, believe, think, be of the opinion, cherish the expectation, desire, imagine, conceive, and confidently suppose, that I am in good health – but I can tell you so to a certainty!

SP: Well that clears that one up. You sound in good spirits.

WAM: You know that I am a great talker.

SP: That's always good news for an interviewer.

WAM: Though my grandmother told my mother, and my mother told her daughter, my sister, that it was a very great art to talk eloquently and well, but an even greater one to know the moment to stop!

SP: May God grant us both that wisdom. But I'm aware you haven't been well recently.

WAM: I've been for a few days confined to the house, and taking antispasmodics, black powders, and elderflower tea as a sudorific.

SP: You're trying to sweat it out?

WAM: I've had a catarrh, a cold in my head, sore throat, headache, pains in my eyes, and earache!

SP: I'm sorry.

WAM: But yesterday I began to take violet syrup and a little almond oil, and already I feel relieved.

SP: Well, I'm very glad to hear it, because I need you fit, and I'd like to start with your travels, for really, Wolfgang, you have been on the road since the age of six. Salzburg was your home in a way – but you've never actually been home!

WAM: I could not endure Salzburg or its inhabitants.

SP: Well, we'll get to this deep antipathy of yours, but first, allow us to travel a little with you. Of course when you were six and seven, you were journeying all over Europe. But when fourteen, you were in Italy with your father, who as ever, was promoting you hard.

WAM: Ah yes, Wolfgang in Germany, Amadeo in Italy!

SP: And you wrote often to your sister Nannerl, who was two years older than you, and a fine musician herself.

WAMM: I would send her a thousand kisses and salutes on her queer monkey face.

SP: And of course you met the Pope in Rome.

WAM: Ah, I really wished that my sister were in Rome, for this city would assuredly have delighted her, because St. Peter's was symmetrical, and many other things in Rome were also symmetrical.

SP: So everything was good in Rome?

WAM: I had one annoyance.

SP: Which was?

WAM: There was only a single bed in our lodgings, so mamma –

SP: – who was back in Salzburg –

WAM: – could easily imagine that I got no rest beside papa.

SP: He snored.

WAM: I truly rejoiced at the thought of a new lodging.

SP: So you lay in bed at night and wrote letters to your sister, with your father beside you, probably trying to get to sleep.

WAM: 'Oh! how I do wish I were as clever and witty as she is!'

I once said. And papa answered, 'So do I'. Then I said, 'Oh! I am so sleepy;' and he merely replied, 'Then stop writing!'

SP: You were hard to slow down even then. You like to fill each moment of the day.

WAM: And I wished to know how Master Canary was.

SP: Your canary in Salzburg?

WAM: Did he still sing? And still whistle?

SP: What made you think of this in Rome?

WAM: Because there was a canary in our anteroom there that chirped out a G sharp just like our one at home.

SP: You were perhaps sometimes a little homesick.

WAM: Naples was beautiful, but as crowded with people as Vienna or Paris. As for London and Naples, I think that the rudeness of the people of Naples almost surpassed that of Londoners.

SP: You must remember, Wolfgang, that I am a Londoner!

WAM: You know I am English at heart!

SP: I'm not sure what you are at heart, Wolfgang; but I'm interested in your travels.

WAM: Naples and Rome are two drowsy cities. The King in Naples had been brought up in the rough Neapolitan fashion, and at the opera always stood on a stool, so that he might look a little taller than the Queen.

sp: Though you weren't tall yourself.

wam: This was true. I had the honour of kissing St. Peter's foot at San Pietro, and as I had the misfortune to be so short, your good old Wolfgang Mozart had to be lifted up!

sp: You're just over five foot, which can sometimes make it hard to gain respect. Did you ever find this?

wam: I remember one rehearsal with the Elector's Orchestra. I could scarcely help laughing when I was presented to the musicians, because, though some knew me by renown and were very civil and courteous, the rest, who knew nothing whatever about me, stared in such a ludicrous way, evidently thinking that because I was little and young, nothing great or mature was to be found in me – but they soon found out.

sp: I'm sure they did. So small a man in stature, but as we know, an enormous letter-writer at this time, keeping your sister and mother informed about what was happening. The one I have here was sent on your mother's name day. Will you read it?

wam: Certainly! 'I wish mamma joy on her name day, and hope that she may live for many hundreds of years to come and retain good health, which I always ask of God, and pray to Him for you both every day. In the meantime, goodbye, mamma. I kiss your hand a thousand times, and remain, till death, your attached son. My prayer to God is that He may grant you health, and allow you to live to be a hundred, and not to die till you are a thousand years old. In the meantime, I hope that you will learn to know me better in future, and that you will then judge me as you please. Time does not permit me to write much. My pen is not worth a pin, nor the hand that guides it.'

SP: I must admit, I do find it hard to read your writing.

WAM: I can't possibly write better, for my pen is only fit to write music and not a letter.

SP: There's something about a violin here in another letter from Italy?

WAM: Let me: 'My violin has been newly strung, and I play every day. I only mention this because mamma wished to know whether I still played the violin. I have had the honour to go at least six times by myself into the churches to attend their splendid ceremonies. In the meantime, I have composed four Italian symphonies, besides five or six arias, and also a motet.'

SP: Not bad for a 14-year-old. And your letter continues –

WAM: 'I am not only still alive, but in capital spirits. Today I took a fancy to ride a donkey, for such is the custom in Italy, so I thought that I too must give it a trial.'

SP: And apart from donkeys, you must have met all sorts on your travels.

WAM: We had the honour once to associate with a certain Dominican who was considered a very pious ascetic.

SP: A truly holy man?

WAM: I somehow don't quite think so, for he constantly took a cup of chocolate for breakfast, and immediately afterwards a large glass of strong Spanish wine!

SP: Interesting.

WAM: And I have myself had the privilege of dining with this holy man, when he drank a lot of wine at dinner and a full glass of very strong wine afterwards, two large slices of melons, some peaches and pears for dessert, five cups of coffee, a whole plateful of nuts, and two dishes of milk and lemons.

SP: It clearly wasn't Lent.

WAM: He may have done this out of bravado, but I don't think so. At all events, it was far too much; and he also ate a great deal for his afternoon snack.

SP: And what did you eat in the heat of Milan?

WAM: Large quantities of fine pears, peaches, and melons.

SP: Because it was warmer than Salzburg.

WAM: Oh, we suffered much from heat in the course of our Italian journey, and the dust constantly dried us up so impertinently that we should have been choked or even died of thirst, had we not been too sensible for that.

SP: And I know the post isn't always reliable, but presumably your mother and sister replied to your letters?

WAM: I told them to address their letters direct to us. It wasn't the custom in Italy, as in Germany, to carry letters round.

sp: They didn't deliver them door to door?

wam: In Italy, we were obliged to go ourselves to fetch them on post days.

sp: And there were always letters waiting for you?

wam: Well, I wished they would answer more punctually, because let's be honest, it's far easier to answer than to originate.

sp: That's interesting, because you've always been energized by other people – and not just in letter-writing. You've needed people around you to spark things, even in composing. Some like to disappear and write alone, but you liked to have others around.

wam: Above us we had a violinist, below us was another, next to us a singing master, who gave lessons, and, in the room opposite, an oboe player.

sp: Sounds like my worst nightmare.

wam: Oh no, this was fabulous for a composer and inspired so many fine thoughts!

sp: And at the age of 15, you met the celebrated opera composer Hasse in Milan – and then promptly outshone him in composition. I know you still have your father's comment which he added to one of your letters home –

wam: 'I am sorry to say that Wolfgang's *Serenata* has totally eclipsed Hasse's opera.'

sp: And to be fair to Hasse, he took the humiliation very well, saying 'This boy will cause us all to be forgotten.' And changing the subject a little: you certainly won't forget the time, Wolfgang. I mean, you seem to own a lot of watches: is there a reason for that?

wam: Most strange that you should say that, for yesterday I was summoned by Count Savioli, to receive my gift. It was just what I had anticipated – a handsome gold watch.

sp: You would have preferred cash.

wam: Ten Carolins would have pleased me better just now, though the watch and chain, with its appendages, are valued at twenty Carolins. Money is what is most needed on a journey; and instead, I now have five watches.

sp: Five? You mean *everyone* gives watches?

wam: Indeed, and I'm seriously considering having a second watch pocket made, and, when I visit a grandee, to wear two watches – which is indeed the fashion here – so that no one may ever again think of giving me another!

sp: You're sick of them.

wam: I must tell you, though, that I do have a genuine Parisian timepiece.

sp: How so?

wam: My jewelled watch, I told you about that.

sp: You said how inferior all the so-called precious stones

were, and how it was a clumsy and awkward shape.

WAM: Indeed. But I wouldn't have cared so much, had I not been obliged to spend quite so much money in repairing and regulating it!

SP: It was high maintenance.

WAM: And after all that, the watch would one day gain a couple of hours, and next day lose in the same proportion! And the one the Elector gave me did just the same, and, if anything, proved even worse and more fragile. So here's what I did: I exchanged these two watches and their chains for a Parisian one which is worth twenty Louis-d'or.

SP: Ahh!

WAM: So now at least I know what time it is, which with my five previous watches, I never knew. I have one I can depend on at last!

SP: Cherish it, Wolfgang, but getting back to travel, the journey from Salzburg to Munich was not one of the better ones.

WAM: A short but disagreeable journey, yes. I do assure you it was impossible for us to sleep for a moment the whole night. The carriage jolted our very souls out, and the seats were as hard as stone! From Wasserburg, I thought I'd never arrive in Munich with whole bones, and during two of the stages, I held on by the straps, suspended in the air and not venturing to sit down.

SP: And of course travel didn't just separate you physically from your family – it also created endless opportunity for misunderstanding. Your mother, for instance, wrote a harsh letter to you on your German tour.

WAM: She made many reproaches in her letters which we did not deserve.

SP: What were her accusations?

WAM: Negligence, thoughtlessness, indolence.

SP: So what did you write back to her?

WAM: I said that we spent nothing but what was absolutely necessary; and as to what was required on a journey, she should know that just as well, if not better, than we did!

SP: You constantly had to justify yourself, to whichever parent you were absent from.

WAM: I told her that no one but myself was responsible for our long stay in Munich; and that had I been alone, I should have stayed there longer.

SP: Really?

WAM: Oh yes. And why were we fourteen days in Augsburg? Because they wished me to give a concert! I was *absolument* determined to leave, but was not allowed, so strong was their desire that I give a concert.

SP: And did you?

WAM: Yes, I gave the concert, and this accounted for the

fourteen days. So the next question: why did we go direct to Mannheim? This I had answered in my previous letter to her. Another question: why were we still in Munich?

sp: Her questions kept coming.

wam: Did she really imagine I'd stay there without good cause? I said. Really, I can only regret your having such an opinion of me, and from my heart grieve, yes, grieve, that you so little know your son! I am not careless, I am only prepared for the worst; so I can wait and bear everything patiently, so long as my honor and the good name of Mozart remain uninjured.

sp: Well, that was telling her! And then of course there was the ten-day journey from Mannheim to Paris, this time with your mother in attendance.

wam: We really thought we wouldn't survive; in my life I never was so wearied. You may easily imagine what it was to leave Mannheim and so many dear kind friends, and then to travel for ten days, not only without these friends, but without any human being – without a single soul whom we could associate with or even speak to.

sp: And it had been hard to leave Mannheim?

wam: I had many kind friends there, both esteemed and rich who wished very much to keep me there.

sp: The place suited you.

wam: Well, where I'm properly paid, I am content to be. Who can tell? It may still come to pass.

sp: You mean proper pay?

wam: I wish it may; and thus it ever is with me – I live always in hope.

sp: The Cannabichs had been kind.

wam: Herr Cannabich was an honorable, worthy man, and a kind friend of mine. He had only one fault.

sp: What was that?

wam: He was rather careless and absent. If you were not constantly before his eyes, he was very apt to forget all about you.

sp: I know people like that.

wam: And I mean, Madame Cannabich and her daughter never gave me a single word of thanks, much less thought of offering me some little gift, however trifling, as a proof of kindly feeling.

sp: A nice watch perhaps?

wam: But nothing of the sort, not even thanks, though I spent many hours teaching the daughter, and took such pains with her. For this they should certainly have thanked me – a truth very well known to all in Mannheim!

sp: But the Webers were more generous – slightly.

wam: Mademoiselle Weber paid me the compliment of kindly knitting two pairs of mits for me, while Monsieur Weber wrote out whatever I required free of charge, gave me the music paper, and also gave me Molière's *Comedies*, as he knew I hadn't read them, with this inscription inside: 'Accept, my dear friend, Molière's works as a token of my gratitude; and sometimes think of me.'

SP: That was kind.

WAM: And when I went away they all wept, and forgive me, but tears come to my eyes even as I think of it. Weber came downstairs with me, and remained standing at the door till I turned the corner and called out 'Adieu!'

SP: Very moving; but then of course you were: moving, moving again, always moving. Though you'll probably tell me it was a good thing.

WAM: Oh, I assure you that people who do not travel, especially artists and scientific men, are but poor creatures. A man of moderate talent will never rise above mediocrity, whether he travels or not, but a man of superior talents, which, without being unthankful to Providence, I cannot deny that I possess, deteriorates if he always remains in the same place.

SP: Maybe, but while there is an excitement and adventure to it all, there is also sadness. Mozart the traveller seems always to have been leaving people.

WAM: As I have told you, leaving Mannheim was sad. But it would have been much more so, had I not from my early youth become quite accustomed to leaving people, countries, and cities. And so with no great expectation of seeing my kind friends either soon or indeed ever again, I left.

TWO

Always the child

---

*I discover many things about Mozart in our brief time together.
I meet Mozart the composer, Mozart the son, Mozart the
performer, Mozart the victim, Mozart the scathing, Mozart the
romantic, Mozart the husband, Mozart the entrepreneur, and
Mozart the penniless. But beneath all these things is Mozart the
eternal child. It was his sister Nannerl who said: 'Outside of
music he was, and remained, nearly always, a child. This was the
chief trait of his character on its shady side; he always needed a
father, mother, or other guardian.'*

*Certainly you could not be with Mozart for long without
experiencing his impish humour. He loves all games, dances,
and, surprisingly perhaps, making masks and costumes. Here is a
hyperactive mind, and we played endless games of billiards, none
of which I won – despite sensing that even as he chalked his cue,
he was composing and orchestrating some new aria in his head.*

*I sensed he felt that he had to be happy; that he was not allowed
to stay morose, but must always be cheerful and optimistic,
with a child's hope in the future. Even when his talk touches on
frustration or unhappiness, it's always balanced with a joke, and
talk of future plans which may make things better. Hope was
always around the corner for Wolfgang; and sadness not a choice.*

SP: You wrote wonderfully playful letters. Here's one to your
cousin –

WAM: Ah yes!

'My dear cousin!

At last I have the honor to inquire how you are, and how you fare? If we soon shall have a talk? If you write with a lump of chalk? If I am sometimes in your mind? If to hang yourself you're inclined? If you're angry with me, poor fool? If your wrath begins to cool? Oh! You are laughing! I knew you could not long resist me, and in your favour would enlist me. Yes! Yes! I know well how this is, though I'm in ten days off to Paris. If you write to me from pity, do so soon from Augsburg city, so that I may get your letter, which to me would be far better.'

SP: I liked the ending as well.

WAM: 'I must conclude, but don't think me rude; he who begins must cease, or the world would have no peace. My compliments to every friend, welcome to kiss me without end, forever and a day, till good sense comes my way; and a fine kissing that will be, which frightens you as well as me. Adieu, ma chère cousine! I am, I was, I have been, oh! That I were, would to heavens I were! I will or shall be, would, could, or should be – what? – a blockhead! W. A. M.'

SP: Your cousin brought out your playfulness.

WAM: Dearest, sweetest, most beauteous, fascinating, and charming of all cousins, most basely maltreated by an unworthy kinsman! Allow me to strive to soften and appease your just wrath, which only heightens your charms and winning beauty, as high as the heel of your slipper! I hope to soften you, Nature having bestowed on me a large amount of softness, and to appease you, being fond of sweet peas.

SP: Though you could be coarse, as in this one here –

I pass it to Wolfgang.

WAM: 'Oh, my arse is burning like fire! I shit on your nose and it will run down your chin! Do you still love me, my dear cousin?'

SP: And surprisingly she did, as did the Cannabichs, with whom you had many a merry night as described in this letter to your father:

WAM: 'I, Johannes Chrisostomus Amadeus Wolfgangus Sigismundus Mozart, am guilty of not coming home until midnight last night – from ten o'clock until the said hour at Cannabich's. I did some rhyming in the presence of said Cannabich, his wife, and daughter. Nothing too serious, rather light and frothy actually, nothing but crude stuff, such as muck, shitting and arse licking, all of it in thoughts and words – but not in deeds! And believe me, I would not have behaved so godlessly if our ring leader known as Lisel – namely Elizabeth Cannabich – had not inspired and excited me so much. I must also confess that I thoroughly enjoyed it all.'

SP: And the confession went on; in a rather unapologetic sort of way.

WAM: 'Yes, I confess all these my sins and shortcomings from the depths of my heart; and in the hope of often having similar ones to confess in the future, I firmly resolve to amend my present sinful life. I therefore beg for a dispensation if it can be granted; but, if not, it is a matter of indifference to me, for the game will go on all the same!'

SP: And of course in another letter, your lack of news leads you on to the subject of the lottery.

WAM: 'I am well, thank God! But have no news, except that in the lottery, the numbers 35, 59, 60, 61, and 62 have turned up prizes, so if we had selected these we should have won; but as we did not put in at all, we neither won nor lost, but merely laugh at those who did the latter.'

SP: You do seem determined to be happy. Perhaps that hides some melancholy?

WAM: Not one of those who knows me can ever say that I was morose or melancholy. I daily thank my creator for such a happy frame of mind.

SP: And you looked to your creator for ultimate assurance.

WAM: Oh yes, I live with God ever before me. I recognize his omnipotence, I fear his anger, I acknowledge his love, and his compassion and mercy towards all his creatures.

SP: And this God is your rock?

WAM: He will never desert those who serve Him.

SP: Really?

WAM: If matters go according to his will, then they go according to mine; consequently nothing can go wrong! And I must be satisfied and happy.

SP: The child who must be happy, and searches always for the rainbow in the rain.

THREE

The Elector's big decision

*From humble beginnings, Leopold Mozart had worked his way
up in the Archbishop of Salzburg's service; but Wolfgang was
never looked on as anything but a servant by the Archbishop,
and treated accordingly. Composers and musicians had no higher
standing than that, which Mozart found humiliating.*

SP: You said that you wished to tell me about your experiences
with the Elector in Mannheim; that I would learn much about
your humiliating life if you did.

WAM: Indeed, so hear this. When in Mannheim, I went to
see Count Savioli, to ask him if it were possible to induce the
Elector to keep me there that winter, as I was anxious to give
lessons to his children. His answer was, 'I will suggest it to the
Elector, and if it depends on me, the thing will certainly be
done.'

SP: You needed the security of a permanent post and Count
Savioli said he would help.

WAM: Indeed, so when the Count saw me on the following
Thursday, he apologized for not having yet spoken to the
Elector, but said that as soon as the gala days were over he
would certainly speak to his Royal Highness.

SP: Encouraging.

WAM: I let three days pass, and, still hearing nothing
whatever, I went to him to make inquiries. He said, 'My good
Mozart, today there was a chassé, so it was impossible for me

to ask the Elector, but tomorrow at this hour I will certainly give you an answer.' I begged him not to forget it.

SP: I'm sure you did.

WAM: To tell you the truth, when I left him I felt rather indignant, so I resolved to take with me the easiest of my six variations of the Fischer minuet, which I wrote here for this express purpose, to present to the young Count, in order to have an opportunity to speak to the Elector myself.

SP: Cunning.

WAM: When I went there, you cannot conceive the delight of the governess, by whom I was most politely received. 'I am so glad that you will stay the winter here,' she said. 'I?' I said. 'But I have not heard a word of it!' 'That does surprise me,' she said, 'for the Elector told me so himself. He said, "By the by, Mozart remains here all winter."'

SP: Excellent!

WAM: Well, we agreed that I should come the next day at four o'clock, and bring some piece of music for the Countess. She was to speak to the Elector before I came; and I should be certain to meet him. So I went that day, but –

SP: But what?

M: He was not there!

SP: Oh my goodness!

M: So I pledged to go the *next* day.

SP: This was dragging on.

WAM: I felt I would most probably spend the winter there, for I was a favourite with his Royal Highness, who thought highly of me, and knew what I could do, and then three days later I was fortunate enough to meet the Elector.

SP: The moment of truth.

WAM: At first, I thought I had again come in vain, as it was so late in the day, but at length we saw him coming. The governess made the Countess seat herself at the piano, and I placed myself beside her to give her a lesson, and it was thus the Elector found us on entering.

SP: Well staged.

WAM: We rose, but he wished us to continue the lesson. When she had finished playing, the governess addressed him, saying that I had written a beautiful Rondo. I played it, and it pleased him exceedingly. At last he said, 'Do you think that she will be able to learn it?' 'Oh! yes,' I said; 'I only wish I had the good fortune to teach it to her myself. So I hope your Highness will place trust and confidence in me.' 'Oh, assuredly,' said he. I thanked him for his present of the watch –

SP: Good move –

WAM: And he said, 'I must reflect on your wish; how long do you intend to remain here?' My answer was, 'As long as your Highness commands me to do so;' and then the interview was at an end.

SP: Oh.

WAM: I went there again the next morning, and was told that the Elector had repeated yesterday, 'Mozart stays here this winter.' Now I was fairly sure it would be so.

SP: And was it? You can't keep me in suspense any longer!

M: The next day Savioli said to me, 'I spoke again yesterday to the Elector, but he has not yet made up his mind.' I then answered, 'I wish to say a few words to you privately;' so we went to the window. I complained of the affair dragging on so long –

SP: – disgraceful treatment –

WAM: – and said how much I had already spent there, entreating him to persuade the Elector to engage me permanently. 'Let him give me work; for I like work.' He said he would certainly suggest it to him, but this evening it was out of the question, as he was not at court; tomorrow, however, he promised me an answer.

SP: A promise you'd heard before.

M: Yes, I began to be rather tired of this joke; I was concerned only to know the outcome. Count Savioli had spoken three times to the Elector, and the answer was invariably a shrug of the shoulders, and 'I will give you an answer presently, but I have not yet made up my mind.'

SP: Frustrating.

WAM: My kind friends all agreed with me in thinking that this hesitation and reserve were rather a favourable omen. For if the Elector was resolved not to engage me, he would have said so at once; so I attributed the delay to him being a little stingy with his money.

s p : I'm feeling impatient just listening.

m : Well, by this time I needed the affair to turn out well; for if not, I would much regret having lingered so long and spent so much money on lodgings. At all events, whatever the outcome was to be, it couldn't be an evil one if it was the will of God – and my daily prayer was that the result would be in accordance with it.

s p : And what was the outcome?

w a m : I went to the court concert a few days later, in the hope of getting an answer. Count Savioli evidently wished to avoid me; but I went up to him, and when he saw me he shrugged his shoulders. 'What!' said I, 'still no answer?' 'Pardon me!' said he, 'but I'm afraid the answer is "No"'

s p : No??

w a m : 'Eh, bien!' said I, 'the Elector might have told me so sooner!' 'True,' said he, 'but he would not even now have made up his mind, if I had not driven him to it by saying that you had already stayed here too long, spending your money in a hotel.' 'Truly, that is what vexes me most of all!' I replied; 'It is very far from pleasant. But, at all events, I am very much indebted to you, Count, for having taken my part so zealously, and I beg you to thank the Elector from me for his gracious, though somewhat tardy information; and I can assure him that, had he accepted my services, he never would have had cause to regret it.'

SP: How blind he was.

WAM: When later I told Cannabich of the debacle, he said, 'I bring you a man who shares the usual happy fate of those who have to do with courts.' 'What!' said his wife, 'So it has all come to nothing?'

SP: They had been hopeful like you were.

WAM: Then Mademoiselle Rose came in and said to me, 'Do you wish me to begin now?' as it was the hour for her lesson. 'I am at your orders,' said I. 'Do you know,' said she, 'that I mean to be very attentive today?' 'I am sure you will,' I answered, 'for sadly the lessons will not continue much longer.' 'How so? What do you mean? Why?' She turned to her mamma, who explained. 'What!' said she, 'is this quite certain? I cannot believe it.' 'Yes, yes; quite certain,' said I. She then played my sonata, but looked very grave. Do you know, I really could not suppress my tears; and by the end, they had all tears in their eyes.

SP: The story does highlight the poor way in which musicians are treated. This was both an expensive and humiliating experience for you.

WAM: Maybe. Though we often think that such and such a thing would be very good, and another thing bad and evil; and yet if these things came to pass, perhaps we'd sometimes learn that the very reverse is the case.

SP: And that, for you, is the rainbow...

FOUR

Death in France

Mozart's mother died while they were together in Paris, where Mozart had been sent by his father to make new contacts. She had not been well for some time. She had complained of ailments in Mannheim, but once in Paris, for the sake of economy, she was exposed to cold and gloomy lodgings. It was not therefore surprising that her health worsened.

This was not Mozart's only trial in France, however, where he seemed to have problems wherever he turned.

SP: Paris was not an easy time for you.

WAM: My father would write saying how I ought to pay a good many visits to make new acquaintances, and to renew former ones. This was impossible, however, with the distances so great – and it was too muddy to go on foot, for really the mud in Paris is beyond all description.

SP: What about a carriage?

WAM: To go in a carriage entailed spending four or five livres a day, and all for nothing!

SP: Nothing?

WAM: Oh, it's true the people say all kinds of civil things, but there it ends. When I play they say 'Oh! c'est un prodige, c'est inconceivable, c'est etonnant!'

SP: And then?

WAM: And then 'Adieu!'

SP: Fine words butter no parsnips.

WAM: At first I spent a lot of money driving about, and to no purpose, for people were often not at home.

SP: A wasted journey.

WAM: Unless you live there, you cannot understand what an annoyance this is. Besides, Paris was much changed; the French were far from being as polite as they had been fifteen years before; their manner bordered on rudeness; and they were odiously self-sufficient.

SP: I suppose the incident with Le Gros didn't help. He seemed to 'lose' a symphony of yours.

WAM: I believed some unseen mischief was at work. I had enemies there – well, where have I not had them? – but that's a good sign.

SP: A good sign, because enemies mean envy means talent. So what happened with the symphony?

WAM: I was obliged to write the symphony very hurriedly, worked hard at it, and the four performers were perfectly enchanted with the piece.

SP: What could possibly go wrong?

WAM: Le Gros then had it for four days to be copied, but I invariably saw it lying in the same place. Then two days later, I couldn't find it at all, though I searched carefully among the music.

sp: Where was it?

wam: Well at last I discovered it hidden away! I took no notice, but said to Le Gros, 'Have you sent my symphony to be copied?' 'Er, no, I forgot all about it,' he said.

sp: He forgot about it? But hadn't he asked you to write it?

wam: As I had no power to compel him to have it transcribed and performed, I said nothing. I then went to the concert when the symphony was due to be performed, only for Ramm and Punto to approach me in the greatest rage to ask why my piece was not being performed. 'I don't know,' I said; 'This is the first I heard of it; I cannot tell.' Well, Ramm was frantic, and abused Le Gros in the music room in French, saying how very unhandsome it was on his part. I alone was to be kept in the dark, it seemed! If he had even made an excuse – that the time was too short, or something of the kind! – but he never uttered a syllable.

sp: So what do you think was going on?

wam: I believe the real cause was Cambini, an Italian maestro; for at our first meeting at Le Gros's, I had unwittingly taken the wind out of his sails.

sp: You do have a sharp tongue. And this was revenge served cold?

wam: If this were a place where people had ears to hear or hearts to feel, and understood just a little of music, and had some degree of taste, these things would only make me laugh heartily, but as it was, so far as music was concerned, I was surrounded there by mere brute beasts.

SP: It was a beastly city.

WAM: There is no place in the world like Paris, believe me, and don't think I exaggerate when I speak in this way of the music there. Ask who you will, anyone – except a Frenchman, of course – and, if trustworthy, you will hear the same.

SP: Though you were offered a post at Versailles which sounds rather fine.

WAM: Yes, Rudolf, who played the French horn, was in the royal service there, and a very kind friend of mine. He offered me the place of organist at Versailles if I chose to accept it.

SP: Was it a good offer?

WAM: The salary would have been 2000 livres a year, but I would have to live six months at Versailles and the remaining six in Paris, or where I pleased.

SP: You didn't take it?

WAM: 2000 livres was no very great sum. It was frightful to see how quickly a dollar went there! And at Versailles, my talents would have been completely buried. Believe me, whoever enters the king's service is forgotten in Paris.

SP: But Paris held darker experiences, because there your mother died.

WAM: Yes.

SP: You didn't tell your father at first, but instead, wrote a letter to him preparing the way, preparing him for the news.

WAM: I told him my dearest mother was very ill; that she has been bled according to her usual custom, which was indeed very necessary.

SP: Did that help?

WAM: It did her much good, yes, but a few days afterwards she complained of shivering and feverishness; then diarrhoea came on and headaches. At first we only used our home remedies, like antispasmodic powders. We would gladly have had recourse to the black powder, of course, but we had none, and could not get it there.

SP: And in the meantime she suffered.

WAM: She became worse every moment, could hardly speak and quite lost her hearing, so that we were then obliged to shout to her, and Baron Grimm sent his doctor to see her.

SP: You felt it was all in the hands of God; or at least that is what you told your father.

WAM: Yes, I firmly believed, and shall never think otherwise, that no doctor, no man living, no misfortune, no casualty, can either save or take away the life of any human being – none but God alone. These are only the instruments that he usually employs – though not always.

SP: How do you mean?

WAM: Well, we sometimes see people swoon, fall down, and

be dead in a moment!

SP: That's true.

WAM: When our time comes, all else is in vain, neither hurrying death nor slowing it. It's about what the Lord wills.

SP: And this thought was consoling for you in the face of this loss.

WAM: I liked to indulge in such consoling thoughts, yes, and, after doing so, felt more cheerful, calm, and tranquil – and you may easily imagine how much I required comfort!

SP: But though you held back the news from your father and sister, you wrote a different letter to your friend Bullinger.

WAM: My dear friend, mourn with me! This is what I said. This has been the most melancholy day of my life; I am now writing at two o'clock in the morning. I must tell you that my mother, my darling mother, is no more. God has called her to himself; I clearly see that it was his will to take her from us, and I must learn to submit to the will of God. The Lord gives, and the Lord takes away. But please – think of all the distress, anxiety, and care I have endured for the last fourteen days. She died quite unconscious, and her life went out like a light. She confessed three days before, took the sacrament, and received extreme unction. The last three days, however, she was in a constant state of delirium, and today, at twenty minutes past five o'clock, her features became distorted and she lost all feeling and perception. I pressed her hand, I spoke to her, but she did not see me and she did not hear me, and all feeling was gone. She lay thus till the moment of her death, twenty past ten at night.

SP: Who else was there?

WAM: There was no one present but myself, Herr Heiner, a kind friend whom my father knew, and the nurse. But I was firmly convinced that it was necessary for her to die, and that God had so ordained it.

SP: So you say. And you asked Bullinger to speak with your father and sister and prepare them for the worst.

WAM: Not to tell them she was actually dead; only prepare them for the truth.

SP: Then a few days later, you wrote to them with the fateful news, and asked them to forgive your 'slight but necessary' deception.

WAM: I told them what I had had to endure, and what courage and fortitude I needed to bear with composure the sight of her daily worsening –

SP: – it's all about Wolfgang so far –

WAM: – how I had suffered and wept, but to what end? Weep, weep, I said myself, as you cannot fail to weep, but take comfort at last; remember that God Almighty has ordained it, and how can we rebel against him?

SP: From a distance, you were trying to calm your father.

WAM: Remember, I said, that she is not lost to us forever, and that we shall see her again, and live together far more happily and blessedly than in this world. The time, as yet, we know not, but that does not disturb me; when God wills it I am ready. Let us therefore pray for her soul, and turn our thoughts to other matters, for there is a time for everything.

SP: And you did turn your thoughts to other matters.

WAM: Of course.

SP: But your father didn't.

WAM: But I could not help laughing heartily at Haydn's tipsy fit.

SP: I beg your pardon?

WAM: My father had told me in his letter that Haydn, organist of the Church of the Holy Trinity, played the organ for the Litany and the *Te Deum Laudamus*, but performed so appallingly that in their shock, they thought he must be paralyzed!

SP: And was he?

WAM: It turned out that he was just rather drunk, so his head and hands did not agree.

SP: A spirited performance.

WAM: And of course this was one of my chief reasons for detesting Salzburg – those coarse, slovenly, dissipated court musicians, with whom no honest man of good breeding could possibly live! It was probably from this very cause that musicians were neither loved nor respected by anyone. In Salzburg, everyone is master; so no one is master.

SP: That's right, because they were at the time missing a musical leader, and there was talk of you returning to Salzburg to take over the orchestra there.

WAM: If I were to become Musical Director there, I would have insisted on exercising complete authority.

SP: And in the meantime, did you meet many composers in France?

WAM: I talked to Piccini at the *Concert Spirituel*; he was always most polite to me and I to him, when we chanced to meet. Otherwise I did not seek much acquaintance, either with him or with any of the other composers; they understood their work and I mine, and that was enough.

SP: Though after your earlier contretemps, relations with the director Le Gros recovered a little.

WAM: Oh yes, Monsieur Le Gros became amazingly well-disposed towards me.

SP: How so?

WAM: I had not been near him for a while, feeling so indignant at my symphony not being performed. Then one day he came into the room and said, 'It is really quite a marvel to have the pleasure of seeing you once more, Mozart.' 'Yes' I said, 'but I have a great deal to do.' 'I hope you will stay and dine with us today?' he says. 'I regret that I cannot,' I reply, 'being already engaged.'

SP: You were playing it cool.

WAM: 'Monsieur Mozart,' he says, 'we really must soon spend a day together.' 'It will give me much pleasure,' I reply. There's a long pause; and then he says: 'I was wondering if you were disposed to write a grand symphony for me for Corpus Christi day?' 'Why not?' I say. 'May I then rely on this?' he asks. 'Oh, yes!' I say, 'if I may, with equal confidence, rely on it being performed, and that it will not fare like my other symphony.'

SP: And what did he say to that broadside?

WAM: Well, this opened the floodgates, and he excused himself in the best way he could, but did not find much to say.

SP: And the outcome?

WAM: In short, the symphony was highly approved of; and Le Gros was very satisfied with it and said it was his very best symphony!

SP: And there were other things to consider while in Paris. Like war, for instance.

WAM: Yes, I had heard that the Emperor had been defeated. At first it was reported that the King of Prussia had surprised the Emperor, or rather the troops of Archduke Maximilian; and that two thousand had fallen on the Austrian side, and that fortunately the Emperor had come to his assistance with forty thousand men, but was then forced to retreat.

SP: That was the news?

WAM: Well, then it was said that the King had attacked the Emperor himself, and entirely surrounded him, and that if General Laudon had not come to his relief with eighteen hundred cuirassiers, he would have been taken prisoner; that sixteen hundred cuirassiers had been killed, and Laudon himself shot dead.

sp: Ah yes, the death of Laudon; I heard about that. How did this death affect you?

wam: For three days I was very depressed and sorrowful. In many ways, it was nothing to me, but I am so sensitive that I feel quickly interested in any matter.

sp: That I can believe.

wam: Still, I then thought it better to have died a glorious death in war than to waste your life in dissipation and vice as too many young men did in Paris. Really, it was worse than ever.

sp: And of course there was a war in France at this time, but it was not of such concern to you. After all, it wasn't your country involved.

wam: The French had recently forced the English to retreat, but it was not a very significant affair. The most remarkable thing was that, friends and foes included, only 100 men were killed.

sp: So you believed it a rather small matter.

wam: Indeed, but in spite of this, there was a great jubilation in Paris, and nothing else was talked of! There was a rumour of peace, but I couldn't have cared less so far as France was concerned.

SP: But for your own country?

WAM: I should indeed be very glad if we could have peace in Germany, for many reasons.

SP: Of course. But meanwhile, war or no war, we must get back to your father, and to your mother's death. He couldn't put it down.

WAM: No, he wished to have an account of her illness and every detail connected with it.

SP: Understandable in a way.

WAM: But I said I'd be brief, and that I'd only allude to the principal facts, as the event was over, and couldn't, alas, be altered. And also, I required some time to discuss business matters with him.

SP: But he felt she could have been saved.

WAM: Yes, so in the first place, I told him that nothing could have saved my mother. No doctor in the world could have restored her to health. It was the clear will of God; her time had come, and God chose to take her to himself.

SP: He thought she'd been bled too long.

WAM: It may have been so, as she did delay it for a little. And I was at that time very anxious to send for another doctor, but she would not allow me to do so, and when I urged her very strongly, she told me that she had no confidence in any French medical man.

SP: A problem when you're in France.

WAM: I therefore looked about for a German one. I could not go out and leave her, however, so waited anxiously for Herr Heiner, who came regularly to see us. But on this occasion, two days passed without his appearing.

SP: And yet you didn't move all that time? That seems strange.

WAM: Well anyway, at last he came, but as our doctor was prevented paying his usual visit the next day, we could not consult with him; in fact, he did not come till the 24th.

SP: So five days on, the German doctor finally appears. Was he good?

WAM: He was about seventy, and gave her rhubarb in wine.

SP: Why am I not reassured?

WAM: I couldn't understand this, as wine is usually thought heating; but when I said so, everyone exclaimed, 'How can you say so? Wine is not heating, but strengthening! Water is heating!' Meanwhile, the poor invalid was longing for a drink of fresh water, and how gladly would I have complied with her wish! But nothing could be done, except to leave her in the hands of the physician.

SP: If you say so.

WAM: All I could do with a good conscience was to pray to God without ceasing, though I went about as if I had gone mad. I mean, I had ample leisure to compose, but I was in such a state that I could not have written a single note!

SP: Proof, if any were needed, of the stress you were feeling.

WAM: On the 26th, the doctor visited her again and imagine my feelings when he suddenly said to me, 'I fear she will scarcely live through the night; she may die at any moment. You had better see that she receives the sacrament.' So I hurried off to find Heiner, knowing that he was at a concert in the house of some count. He said that he'd bring a German priest with him next morning.

SP: Not exactly rushing.

WAM: Then on my way back, I looked in briefly on Madame d'Epinay and Monsieur Grimm as I passed. They were distressed that I had not spoken sooner, as they would at once have sent their doctor. I did not tell them my reason, of course, which was that my mother would not see a French doctor.

SP: That must have been awkward.

WAM: It was awkward, yes, as they then said they would send their physician that very evening! But when I got home, I told my mother that I had met Herr Heiner with a German priest – who had heard a great deal about me and was anxious to hear me play – and that they were both to call on us next day. She seemed quite satisfied, and though I was no doctor, seeing that she was better I said nothing more.

SP: And so that was the story, up until your mother's final decline. Perhaps your father harassed you so much because he felt guilty? After all, he had sent her to France with you. But you now wished to move on and told your father so.

WAM: All is over, I said, and were we to write whole pages on the subject, we could not alter that simple fact.

SP: And in the meantime, you had to think about money again, because you found it hard to get paid in France. You either felt people were trying it on – or simply not taking you seriously.

WAM: What provoked me most of all was those stupid Frenchmen thinking I was still only seven years old, as they had seen me first when I was that age.

SP: When you toured as a child.

WAM: I knew this was so, for Madame d'Epinay told me. I was therefore treated like a beginner – except by the musicians, obviously, who thought very differently. But you know what they say – the most votes carry the day!

SP: And in the meantime?

WAM: In the meantime, my plan was to do my utmost to gain a livelihood by teaching, and to earn as much money as possible, in the fond hope that some change may soon occur.

SP: And things needed to change.

WAM: I cannot deny, and indeed frankly confess, that I'd have been delighted to be free of that place. Giving lessons there was no joke, and unless you wore yourself out by taking a number of pupils, not much money could be made.

SP: And it also left no time for composition.

WAM: No, my mode of life prevented this. I had some hours

at liberty, but those few hours were more necessary for rest than for work.

SP: I understand; though surprisingly, when your stay in France came to the end, you were actually a bit slow in returning home. Why was that – when you hated it there?

WAM: There never was any other cause for my long delay but a fear which gave rise to a feeling of sadness that I could no longer conceal.

SP: You feared your father?

WAM: What other cause could I possibly have? Yet I had done nothing to give him reason to reproach me; I was guilty of no fault; and by a fault I mean something which does not become a Christian and a man of honour.

SP: And I suppose although Salzburg was home, it wasn't home. You'd hardly lived there.

WAM: No, no, I rejoiced and anticipated the most agreeable and happy days there – but only in the company of my father and my dear sister. Salzburg and its inhabitants, I could not endure.

SP: All of them?

WAM: I speak of the natives of Salzburg. Their language and manners are to me quite intolerable.

SP: And as we leave France, there was another death in that country while you were there, and one which you had rather different feelings about. The atheist Voltaire passed away.

WAM: The ungodly arch-villain died miserably like a dog; just like a brute. This was his reward!

FIVE

Father and son

*In our conversations, the relationship between father and son
comes up again and again.*

*Leopold was a gifted musician himself, and had written a book
on violin-playing which sold across Europe. But after guiding
Wolfgang's musical education, Leopold found it hard to let go of
the reins, and he was forever telling him what he ought to do.
Having lost five children, Leopold clearly looked to his remaining
two, Nannerl and Wolfgang, to make money and look after him.
'Only a saint would expect no return on his investment of time
and energy,' said one friend.*

*Wolfgang determinedly praises his father in his letters. But it was
a constant pain that as far as his father was concerned, nothing
Wolfgang ever did seemed good enough, and nothing he ever did
seemed right.*

*The interdependence between them meant that any estrangement
seemed only temporary to Wolfgang; he couldn't see that it was
permanent.*

SP: You speak often of God, Wolfgang.

WAM: Indeed.

SP: And you speak often of your father.

WAM: Of course.

SP: Was it perhaps hard sometimes to distinguish between the voice of God and that of your father?

WAM: I certainly worked hard to live as strictly as possible in accordance with my father's injunctions and advice.

SP: And his advice was never slow in coming.

WAM: Parents strive to place their children in a position which shall enable them to earn their own living; and this they owe to their children and the state. The greater the talents with which the children have been endowed by God, the more are they bound to make use of those talents to improve the conditions of themselves and their parents, to aid their parents and to care for their own present and future welfare. We are taught thus to trade with our talents in the Gospels. I owe it, therefore, to God and my conscience to pay the highest gratitude to my father, who tirelessly devoted all his hours to my education, and to lighten his burdens.

SP: A grand speech. But did you perhaps feel that you were never quite good enough?

WAM: I earnestly begged him to go on loving me a little, yes, just until I could open new shelves in my small and confined knowledge-box, where I could stow away the good sense which I had every intention to acquire.

SP: Your father accused you of losing your religion.

WAM: I was rather vexed by one inquiry.

SP: Which was that?

WAM: He asked if I had perhaps forgotten to go to confession.

SP: How did you respond?

WAM: I said that I'd not say anything further on the matter!

SP: Which is usually a sign you're about to.

WAM: Only that he should allow one request, which was: not to think so badly of me! I like to be merry, but rest assured that I can be as serious as anyone. Since I left Salzburg, and even in Salzburg, I have met with people who spoke and acted in a way that I personally should have felt ashamed of, even though they were ten, twenty, even thirty years older than myself! I implored him, most earnestly, to have a better opinion of me.

SP: But I wonder if he did? On another occasion he told you to remember you had an immortal soul.

WAM: Well, as for that, not only did I think this, but I firmly believed in it! Were it not so, how would men be any different from animals?

SP: I can see why you found it hard to open your heart to your father.

WAM: I would gladly have opened my heart to him, but was deterred by the reproaches I dreaded.

SP: You received a difficult letter from him in 1778.

WAM: 'Next to God comes papa' was my axiom when a child and I still think the same.

SP: But on this occasion, he thought you were spending too

much time in Mannheim, and spending too much money there, while back in Salzburg he was dressed in rags. And his feelings shocked you.

WAM: Yes, I was so shocked at these words that tears came to my eyes on reading that letter, saying he goes about so shabbily dressed.

SP: How did you respond?

WAM: 'My very dearest papa, this is certainly not my fault,' I said. 'You know it is not! We economize in every possible way here; food and lodging, wood and light cost us nothing, and as for dress, you are well aware that in places where you are not known, it is out of the question to be badly dressed, for appearances must be kept up!'

At that time, my hopes centered on Paris, for I could see the German princes were all skinflints. And I meant to work with all my strength, that I might soon have the joy of extricating my father from his distressing circumstances.

SP: We've talked of Paris. You were originally to go there with the Wendlings. This is what your father wished, but you decided against it. Why?

WAM: Mamma and I discussed the matter, and we agreed that we did not like the sort of life the Wendlings led.

SP: What sort of life was that?

WAM: Wendling was a very honourable and kind man, but unhappily devoid of all religion and the whole family was the same. His daughter was a most disreputable character, and though Ramm was a good fellow, he was a libertine, and I was alarmed even at the very thought of being in the society of people whose mode of thinking was so entirely different from mine, and indeed, from that of all good people.

sp: You condemned them in your mind.

wam: They could do as they pleased, but I had no heart to travel with them, nor could I enjoy one pleasant hour, nor indeed know what to talk about. Friends who had no religion could not long be our friends.

sp: But weren't you being a bit sparing with the truth here? The real reason you didn't wish to go to Paris was that you had other plans. You had fallen in love with the daughter of your new friend Herr Weber – but couldn't tell your father this.

wam: When I was with Herr Weber, it was just as if I were with my father. This was the reason I liked him so much; same mode of thinking, and if my mother had not been too comfortably lazy to write, she would have backed me up on this. I was so attached to this oppressed family that my greatest wish was to make them happy. My advice was that they should go to Italy.

sp: And Aloysia? What did you think of her?

wam: Mademoiselle Weber, like my sister in Salzburg, enjoyed the best reputation, owing to the careful way in which she had been brought up.

sp: But when you told him about going to Italy with her, to make her a prima donna, he thought you were mad. Indeed, I have the letter, a rather forthright one, which I think you might remember.

WAM: I do indeed: 'The object of your journey,' he said, 'was to assist your parents, and to contribute to your dear sister's welfare, but, above all, that you might acquire honour and fame in the world, which you in some degree did in your boyhood. And now it rests entirely with you to raise yourself by degrees to one of the highest positions ever attained by any musician. This is a duty you owe to a kind Providence in return for the remarkable talents with which He has gifted you; and it depends wholly on your own good sense and good conduct, whether you become a commonplace artist whom the world will forget, or a celebrated musical director of whom posterity will read of hereafter in books; whether, infatuated with some pretty face, you one day breathe your last on a straw sack, your wife and children in a state of starvation, or, after a well-spent Christian life, die peacefully in honour and independence, and your family well-provided for. Get off to Paris without delay. Take your place by the side of really great people. Aut Caesar aut nihil!

SP: 'Either Caesar or nothing'. Strong words from your father. And your mother added a bit at the end of your letter that week, which you didn't see before she sent it. Can you read it?

WAM: Yes, she wrote this: 'No doubt you perceive by the accompanying letter that when Wolfgang makes new friends he would give his life for them. It is true that Aloysia does sing incomparably; still, we ought not to lose sight of our own interests. I never liked his being in the society of Wendling and Ramm, but I did not venture to object to it, nor would he have listened to me; but no sooner did he get to know these Webers, than he instantly changed his mind. In short, he prefers other people to me, for I remonstrate with him sometimes, and he doesn't like it. I write this quite secretly while he is at dinner, for I don't wish him to know it.'

SP: So perhaps you used talk of the godless Wendlings to block the journey to France; and contrary to what you say, your mother wasn't in on the plan at all.

WAM: These things are not important.

SP: But in the meantime, really, what a mess! Your father wanted you to go to Paris, and earn some money. You wanted to go to Italy with the Webers – and in particular, with Aloysia.

WAM: I knew that he would disapprove of my journey with the Webers. I wish my position had been such that I had no cause to consider anyone else, and that we were all independent; but in the intoxication of the moment, I forgot the present impossibility of the affair, and also to tell him what I had done.

SP: You are perhaps not as confident as you appear.

WAM: When people lose confidence in me, I am apt to lose confidence in myself.

SP: You hide that vulnerability.

WAM: And I told my father that the days when I sang standing on a stool and at the end of the performance kissed the tip of his nose, they were gone; but that he still had my reverence, love, and obedience. I say no more.

SP: And Aloysia as a singer at this time?

WAM: I confess I was an ass.

SP: Really?

WAM: She did not even know what singing meant. It was true that, for a person who had only been learning music for three months, she sang surprisingly; and, besides, she had a pleasing and pure voice. The reason why I praised her so much was probably my hearing people say, from morning to night, 'There is no better singer in all Europe; those who have not heard her have heard nothing!'

SP: That's what people said?

WAM: And I did not venture to disagree with them, partly because I wished to acquire friends, and partly because I had come direct from Salzburg, where we are not in the habit of contradicting anyone. But as soon as I was alone, I never could help laughing.

SP: Why, then, did you not laugh at her in your letter to your father?

WAM: I really cannot tell.

SP: Perhaps you were afraid of him. He did tend to believe the worst of you.

WAM: Yes! So believe what you will about me, I said, only nothing bad, nothing bad! There are people who think no one can love a poor girl without evil designs. But I am a Mozart; and, though young, still a high-principled Mozart! So pardon me if, in my eagerness, I became somewhat excited. I might have said a great deal more on this subject, but I couldn't.

SP: Why not?

WAM: I felt it to be impossible. Among my many faults is the belief that those friends who know me, do so thoroughly. And in that instant, many words are not necessary.

SP: A sharp riposte to your father.

M: No, not aimed at my dearest papa.

SP: Really?

WAM: No! He understood me too well, and was too kind to try to deprive anyone of their good name. I only meant it for those who could believe such a thing of me.

SP: I see.

WAM: Though I did ask him not to write me any more melancholy letters, for I required a cheerful spirit, a clear head, and inclination to work; and such are not possible for one who is sad at heart.

SP: His letters made you sad.

WAM: I knew, and, believe me, felt deeply, just how much he deserved rest and peace, but was I an obstacle to this? I would not willingly be so, and yet, alas! I feared I was.

SP: He felt you weren't supporting him properly; but you still had this dream of you all living together eventually.

WAM: I said that if I attained my object, which was to live respectably in Munich or Vienna, he must instantly leave

Salzburg. We could all live together. I had a roomy alcove in my first room in Mannheim, in which two beds stood. These would do splendidly for him and me. As for my sister, we could perhaps put a stove into the next room, which would only cost four or five florins.

SP: So she'd have a warm room.

WAM: And as for my room, well, we could heat the stove till it was red-hot and leave the stove door open into the bargain – and it would still be unendurable! It was so frightfully cold in Mannheim.

SP: And it wasn't just melancholy letters he sent. In your own inimitable fashion, you also rebuked him for writing short letters. Read what you wrote. I like this opening of yours –

WAM: 'I have this moment received your few lines of January 1st. When I opened the letter I chanced to hold it in such a manner that nothing but a blank sheet met my eyes. At last I found your writing.'

SP: Aooww!

SIX

The art of composition

Mozart needed no formal lessons in composition. He'd been at it since the age of five, and possessed astonishing powers of assimilation through watching, hearing and reading music. He could mimic styles, and his travels gave him plenty to imitate – whether sacred, dramatic or instrumental. As he said to me: 'I can pretty well adapt or conform myself to any style of composition.'

Mozart learned much from Johann Christian Bach whom he met in London as a child, and admired greatly. In the early 1780s, he was introduced to the work of his father, Johann Sebastian Bach, another great influence, as was the tutelage of Padre Martini in Bologna, where Wolfgang learned the discipline of counterpoint – the use of two or more melodies simultaneously.

Mozart composed – or as he would call it, 'speculated' – while walking up and down, revolving musical ideas in his mind and forming them into orderly mental compositions. This meant that the subsequent transcription of the music onto paper was a slightly mechanical occupation, which required little effort. It was already perfect in his head; and it was in his head and imagination that he was transported to the sweet realm of tones, far from the miseries of this world.

Neither was he just concerned with the music. The opera Idomeneo, King of Crete, *composed in 1778, revealed how seriously he treated the text. He told me that he kept cutting the speech of the sea god. I asked him why, and he explained that the shock of hearing the divine voice quickly loses its effect. 'If the speech of the ghost in* Hamlet *were not so long, it would be much more effective.'*

Maybe even the great English bard could have learned something from this cocky young German.

SP: Is it true that one evening you apparently composed a clarinet trio in your head while playing skittles with some drinking chums?

WAM: I compose as a sow piddles!

SP: Well, that's one way of putting it. So new music comes to you seemingly unbidden, complete in every detail?

WAM: I know all the airs thoroughly by heart, so I can see and hear them in my own thoughts at home. You know, though, my greatest desire is to write operas.

SP: Yes, but you turned down an opera once.

WAM: It was a miserable piece –

SP: You mean the text?

WAM: Whoever composed music for it without changing the text entirely ran a great risk of being hooted off the stage. Even with the finest music no one could have tolerated such a piece. As it turned out, the music was terrible also, so I don't know whether the author or the composer should carry off the prize for inanity.

SP: And you say you're writing two concertos at the moment.

WAM: These concertos are a happy medium between being too easy and too difficult. They are very bright, pleasant to the ear, and natural without being vacuous.

s p: So all can enjoy them?

wa m: There are certain passages for the connoisseurs alone
to enjoy, but I still believe the less learned cannot fail to be
pleased, even perhaps without knowing why.

s p: It's about trying to please everyone; finding the happy
medium perhaps?

wa m: The happy medium is the truth in all things, certainly
– but is no longer known or valued.

s p: Really?

wa m: To gain applause these days, one must write things so
crass that they might happily be played on barrel organs!

s p: And this has been a problem: your music is too highbrow.
I have here a letter from your father in which he says that
you're not to think only of the musical public in your work,
but also of the unmusical. 'You know that there are a hundred
ignorant people for every ten true connoisseurs,' he says, 'so do
not forget what is called 'popular' and tickle the long ears' – by
which he presumably means the donkeys!

wa m: 'As to the matter of popularity,' I replied, 'be
unconcerned, papa; there is music in my opera for all sorts of
persons – though none for donkeys.'

s p: But Hofmeister, the Leipzig publisher, agreed with your
father. He said to you, 'Mozart, write in a more popular style
or I can neither print nor pay for anything of yours.'

wa m: 'Very well!' I said, 'then I shall earn nothing more, go hungry and the devil a bit will I care!'

SP: But of course you *did* care.

WAM: My friend, melody is the essence of music.

SP: And you do write good melodies.

WAM: I compare a good melodist to a fine racer, and counter pointists to hack post-horses.

SP: You think we complicate things.

WAM: Remember the old Italian proverb: 'Who knows most, knows least.'

SP: True. But of course your music is not just simple melody. Some of it really is quite complicated. In 1785, you dedicated six quartets to Haydn. But they were so full of unfamiliar chords and dissonances that the publishers sent them back, thinking they must be errors!

WAM: Huh!

SP: And then Grassalkowitsch, the Hungarian prince, thought his musicians were getting it wrong in some of the passages, and when he learned they were only playing the music in front of them, he tore the music to pieces!

WAM: Those pieces are, indeed, the fruit of long and painstaking labour.

SP: And not immediately appreciated.

WAM: But my friends encouraged me in the hope that my work would be rewarded, which gave me courage, yes – and perhaps the flattering belief that these, my offspring, would some day bring me comfort.

SP: Well, this score in my hand has certainly brought comfort – a lovely quintet you wrote in 1784, for oboe, clarinet, French horn, bassoon, and piano.

WAM: Ahh! Well, that one was received with extraordinary applause and I considered it then the best thing I had ever composed in my life.

SP: So tell me – can anyone learn to be a composer? I mean, could I be a composer?

WAM: If one has the talent it pushes for utterance and torments you; it will out.

SP: But I can't learn it from a book?

WAM: There is nothing in this business which can be learned from a book. Here, here, and here – (*he points to his ear, his head, and his heart*) is your school. If everything is right there, then take your pen and write it down. And then, of course, ask the opinion of a man who knows his business.

SP: Perhaps everything comes more easily to you than others? Everything seems easy to the prodigy.

WAM: It's a mistake to think that my art has become easy to me. I assure you, dear friend, no one has given so much care to the study of composition as I. There is scarcely one famous master in music whose works I have not frequently and diligently studied. One thing is certain, though –

SP: What's that?

WAM: I must compose a great opera or none.

SP: Because?

WAM: Well, in France, if I wrote only smaller ones, I received very little, for there, everything was done at a fixed price, and if it turned out the obtuse French didn't like it, then that was that!

SP: You got nothing?

WAM: I'd get no more commissions, have very little profit, and find my reputation damaged. If, on the other hand, I could write a great opera, the remuneration is better, and I'm working in my own peculiar sphere, the one in which I delight, and have a greater chance of being appreciated – because in a great work there is more opportunity to gain approval.

SP: Of course you didn't much like the French language.

WAM: It's true that the devil himself invented that language, and I quite saw the difficulties which all composers have found in it. But, in spite of that, I felt myself as able to surmount those difficulties as anyone else. Indeed, I felt quite a fiery impulse within me, and trembled from head to foot with desire to teach those French more fully how to know and value and fear the Germans!

SP: Yes, not all wars involve guns.

WAM: If it ran its course without a duel, I should have preferred it, for I do not care to wrestle with dwarfs.

SP: The French experience must have been harder for all the success you'd had previously. After all, you were only seventeen when an opera of yours went down so splendidly in Munich.

WAM: Yes, and it proved so successful that I cannot possibly describe all the tumult.

SP: Well, try.

WAM: In the first place, the whole theatre was so crammed that many people were obliged to go away. After each aria there was invariably a tremendous uproar and clapping of hands, and cries of 'Viva Maestro!'

SP: Very gratifying.

WAM: Her Serene Highness the Electress and the Dowager, who were opposite me, also called out 'Bravo!'

SP: Even the Royals loved you.

WAM: Then when the opera was over – during the interval when all is usually quiet till the ballet begins – the applause and shouts of 'Bravo!' were renewed!

SP: And this went on?

WAM: Sometimes there was a lull, but only to recommence afresh, and so forth. And I went afterwards with papa to a room through which the Elector and the whole court were to pass. I kissed the hands of the Elector and the Electress and the other royalties, who were all very gracious.

SP: I'm not surprised you were excited in your letter home.

WAM: I kissed mamma 1,000,000,000 times – I didn't have room for any more noughts – and a thousand kisses for Miss Bimber the dog, and as for my sister, well, I would rather have embraced her in person than in my imagination.

SP: And being away from home so much in your early years, imagination was often all you had. As a child, you say you invented an entire imaginary world on long carriage trips. And did you perhaps imagine success in Italy? For Italy was surely the Holy Grail for musicians. And you'd had good experiences there as a teenager.

WAM: When I come to reflect on the subject, in no country have I received such honours, or been so esteemed, as in Italy, and it's true, nothing contributes more to a man's fame than to have written Italian operas. In Italy, one could gain more honour and credit with one opera, than with one hundred concerts in Germany.

SP: We're back with operas.

WAM: Yes, even back then, I had the most ardent desire to write another opera. When I heard an opera being discussed, or was in a theatre myself and heard the singing, Oh! I really was beside myself!

SP: But you don't rush in. You like to tailor work to individuals

WAM: I do. And I remember taking Herr Raaff an aria that I

had written for him.

sp: Did he like it?

wam: The aria pleased him beyond all measure, but I told
him to speak frankly if it did not suit his voice or please him,
for I would alter it if he wished, or indeed write another.
'Heaven forbid!' he exclaimed – 'it must remain just as it is, for
nothing can be more beautiful. I only wish you to shorten it
a little, for I am no longer able to sustain my voice through so
long a piece.' 'Most gladly,' I answered. I had deliberately made
it rather long, you see, for it's always easy to shorten something
– but not so easy to lengthen.

sp: So the aria was made to fit Raaff.

wam: I think an aria should fit a singer as accurately as a well-
made coat.

sp: Though I suppose there are other reasons for change in the
rehearsal process. You were telling me about preparations of
your opera *Idomeneo*.

wam: Well, there the scene between father and son in the first
act, and the first scene in the second act, were both too long
and sure to weary the audience, particularly as in the first one,
the actors were both bad, and in the second, another was also
very inferior. So if the librettist hadn't cut them, then I would
have done, for the scenes could not remain as they were.

sp: And the Elector listened to the rehearsal on that occasion?

wam: Yes, and after the first act he called out 'Bravo!' And
rather too audibly!

SP: Well don't sound so pleased!

WAM: And later, laughing, he said to me: 'Who could believe that such great things could be hidden in so small a head?'

SP: A compliment that perhaps only an Elector could get away with. But it wasn't all applause and 'bravo!' in the world of music. I heard a rather dark story about the musician Marquesi. Indeed, it could almost be an opera in itself.

WAM: Ah yes, well you probably know that the worthy Marquesi was poisoned in Naples, but how?

SP: I was hoping you'd tell me.

WAM: Well, he was in love with a Duchess, whose rightful lover became jealous, and sent three or four fellows to give him the choice between either drinking poison out of a cup or being assassinated.

SP: Neither really appeals.

WAM: He chose the former –

SP: – drinking the poison –

WAM: – so being an Italian poltroon he died alone, and allowed his murderers to live on in peace and quiet!

SP: I hadn't thought of that.

WAM: I would at least have taken a couple with me into the next world, if absolutely obliged to die myself. Such an admirable singer is a great loss.

s p: Indeed. And so getting back to composition, does the subject matter of an opera affect your choice?

w a m: I don't care what the subject matter is, provided the libretto is good.

s p: But it affects the style of music?

w a m: Do you really suppose I am likely to write a comic opera in the same style as a serious one?

s p: I was only asking.

w a m: There should be as little levity in a serious opera, and as much learning and solidity, as there should be as little learning in a comic opera.

s p: But I suppose no one wants *all* serious – even in serious.

w a m: That people like to have a little comic music in serious opera, I cannot help.

s p: And how do you relate music to emotion? I heard one aria the other day and noticed that you used quick notes to denote increasing anger.

w a m: As a man in a violent fit of passion transgresses all the bounds of order and propriety, and forgets himself in a fury, the same must be the case for the music too.

s p: I see.

w a m: But just as the passions must never be expressed so as to become revolting, so the music in even the most appalling of situations, should never offend the ear, but continue to please and be melodious. So in the aria you mention, I did not go from F, in which the air is written, into a remote key, but into an analogous one; not into its nearest relative D minor, but into the more remote A minor.

SP: I'll take your word for it.

WAM: Or take 'O wie Ängstlich, O wie feurig,' –

SP: Oh how fearful, Oh how fiery!

WAM: And the 'throbbing heart' which I could express in octaves on the violin. This is the favourite aria of all those who have heard it, and mine also.

SP: Really?

WAM: You hear the trembling, throbbing, swelling breast expressed by a crescendo, while the whispers and sighs are rendered by the first violins with mute and a flute in unison.

SP: The composer's secrets.

WAM: In an opera, though, the poetry must necessarily be the daughter of the music. Why do the Italian comic operas go down well everywhere, with all their wretched poetry – yes, even in Paris? Because music rules supreme, and all else is forgotten.

SP: So the music comes first – though people do like a good plot.

WAM: An opera is certain to become popular when the plot

is well worked out; but always with the verse written expressly for the music, and not merely to suit some miserable rhyme.

sp: So no rhymes for rhyme's sake.

wam: This practice brings in words and even entire verses which completely ruin the ideas of the composer. Rhyming for rhyming's sake is most pernicious.

sp: As is vertigo.

wam: Vertigo?

sp: I mention this for a reason, because you had some medical advice for your father, when he was suffering from it.

wam: Certainly.

sp: It's a bit off our subject, I know, but there's more to life than music, and I'm so interested in medical advances. Your advice for vertigo –

wam: – I had been assured my ideas were certain to have a good effect –

sp: – indeed, so what was it?

wam: I told my father to take some cart grease, wrap it in paper, and wear it on his chest.

sp: I'd never have thought of that.

wam: Then bruise the bone of a leg of veal, and add a little leopard's bane, and carry it in the pocket. I hoped this would certainly cure him.

S P: Your gifts are wasted in music, Wolfgang. You should have been a doctor! And tell me – as a master of composition, is that a good way to end this act?

WA M: No, no! The close must make a great deal of noise; that's all that is necessary for the end of an act. In fact, the noisier the better and the shorter the better, so that the audience do not get too cool to applaud!

SEVEN

The ups and downs of piano lessons

*Short, pale, and insignificant in appearance, Mozart excites
audiences – but struggles to interest either aristocratic or
ecclesiastical patrons as a serious composer. He's never found an
official post that pays well enough to allow him to concentrate on
composing. This means he spends much of his time giving piano
lessons, which have had their ups and downs.*

SP: You have been a piano tutor to many young people.

WAM: With regard to the daughter of Hamm, the Secretary
of War, there could be no doubt she had a decided talent for
music, for she had only learned three years, and could play a
number of pieces very well.

SP: Her technique was good?

WAM: I didn't know what to make of her. She seemed to me
so curiously constrained, and possessed such an odd way of
stalking over the keys with her long bony fingers. Up to now,
of course, she'd had no really good teacher, and if she had
remained in Munich she'd never have become what her father
wished and hoped.

SP: And what was that?

WAM: Oh, he was eager beyond measure that she should one
day be a distinguished pianist!

SP: Another pushing parent. And did you push her?

WAM: I really could not for laughing, for when I occasionally played something with the right hand, she instantly said 'bravissimo!' in the voice of a little mouse.

SP: And then there was Nanette, aged 8.

WAM: Anyone who can see and hear her play without laughing must be made of stone, like her father.

SP: Where's the comedy?

WAM: She perches herself exactly opposite the treble, avoiding the centre, that she may have more room to throw herself about and make grimaces. She rolls her eyes and smirks; and when a passage comes twice she always plays it slower the second time, and if three times, slower still.

SP: She sounds like a bit of a drama queen.

WAM: She raises her arms when playing a passage, and if it is to be played with emphasis, she seems to give it with her elbows and not with her fingers, as awkwardly and heavily as possible. The funniest thing is that when a passage should flow like oil, and the fingers must necessarily be changed, she does not pay much heed to that.

SP: No?

WAM: But rather lifts her hands, and quite coolly goes on again. This, of course, makes a wrong note more than likely, and I say this only in order to give you some idea of piano-playing and teaching, so that you may in turn derive some benefit from it.

sp: Of course. I'm eager to find a teacher and start learning.

wam: Nanette's father was quite infatuated with his daughter, and she may one day be clever, for she has genius, but as things stand, she'll never improve, nor will she ever acquire much velocity of finger, for her present method is sure to make her hand heavy. And she will never master what is the most difficult, necessary, and in fact the *principal* thing in music.

sp: And what is that, maestro?

wam: Time.

sp: Time?

wam: Time – because from her infancy she has never been in the habit of playing in correct time. Herr Stein and I discussed this point together for at least two hours.

sp: Herr Stein the piano maker?

wam: He asked my advice on every subject. I mean, he was quite devoted to Becke, but then he saw and heard that I could do more than Becke; that I made no grimaces along the way and yet played with so much more expression.

sp: He was a convert?

wam: He duly acknowledged that none of his acquaintances – no, not one – had ever handled his pianos as I did.

sp: So clearly you keep good musical time?

wam: The way I keep in time so accurately causes them all

much surprise.

sp: What's the secret?

wam: The left hand being quite independent, they cannot understand at all!

sp: So it's all about the independent left hand.

wam: With them, the left hand always yields to the right. Count Wolfeck – who also had a passionate admiration for Becke – recently said that in a concert, I beat Becke hollow.

sp: Oh!

wam: No really, Count Wolfeck went round the room saying, 'In my life, I never heard anything like this.'

sp: So did you bow quietly and retire for the night?

wam: No, I played some more!

sp: Shameless!

wam: And what a noise and commotion there was! Herr Stein did nothing but make faces and grimaces of astonishment. Herr Demmler was seized with fits of laughter, for he was a queer creature, and when deep in pleasure, laughed very heartily; indeed, on this occasion he actually began to swear!

sp: And getting away from you and back to your pupils for a moment, Mademoiselle Rosel? She was another one.

wam: Mademoiselle Rosel was very clever, and learned with

ease. Her right hand was very good, but the left was sadly quite ruined. And I must say that I did really feel very sorry for her, when I saw her labouring away till she was actually panting for breath.

sp: Why was that?

wam: Being so accustomed to this method, she could not play in any other way, never having been shown the right one. I said – both to her mother and herself – that if I were her regular master I would lock up all her music, cover the keys of the piano with a handkerchief, and make her exercise her right and left hand, at first quite slowly, until her hands were thoroughly trained.

sp: And after that?

wam: And after that I should feel confident of making her a genuine pianist. They both acknowledged that I was right, of course. But in the meantime, it was a sad pity; for she had so much genius, read music very tolerably, had great natural aptitude, and played with considerable feeling.

sp: But she'd learned bad habits and these held her back. You must have helped a lot of young musicians.

wam: Indeed. But in many ways, tutoring piano pupils is a form of work that does not suit me.

sp: Why not?

wam: I am willing to give lessons out of deference, especially when I see genius, or an inclination and anxiety to learn. But to be obliged to go to a house at a certain hour, or else to wait at home, is what I cannot submit to.

SP: And I suppose quite often you'd turn up at the house and they wouldn't be there.

WAM: In which case, let me tell you, I wouldn't return.

SP: Once bitten –

WAM: – no, I found it impossible, so had to leave tutoring to those who can do nothing but play the piano. I am, after all, a composer, and born to become a Musical Director, and neither can I, nor ought I bury my talent for composition, with which God has so richly endowed me.

SP: That's how you feel.

WAM: And I say this without arrogance –

SP: – quite –

WAM: – for I feel it now more than ever. I would rather neglect the piano than composition, for I look on the piano to be only a secondary consideration; though, thank God, a very strong one too.

SP: And this frustration perhaps struck you most forcefully in France? Your piano lessons were taking you away from composing.

WAM: Giving lessons there was no fun; you had to work yourself pretty tired, and if you didn't give a good many lessons, you would make but little money. And you mustn't think that was laziness.

SP: The thought never crossed my mind.

WAM: It just went counter to my genius, counter to my mode of life. You know how I am wrapped up in music, that I practice it all day long, that I like to speculate, study, consider. Yet all this was prevented by my mode of life there.

SP: The endless lessons.

WAM: I mean, I had some free hours, but they were necessary more for recuperation than work.

EIGHT

Mozart and his women

Pampered by women when a child, Mozart has remained precociously aware of their looks for the rest of his life.

SP: People often think ill of you in your relationship with women.

WAM: Pray believe anything you please about me, but nothing ill.

SP: It's all right; I'm not your father.

WAM: There are persons who believe it's impossible to love a poor girl without harbouring wicked intentions. I am a Mozart, but a young and well-meaning Mozart, and among my many faults is the belief that the friends who know me, know me.

SP: Hence words of explanation are not needed.

WAM: And if they do not know me, where shall I find words enough?

SP: Point taken. So I'm not asking you to justify yourself – merely to hear your side of the story. You were fond of your cousin, Maria, for instance, and she was fond of you, as your letters reveal.

WAM: My cousin was pretty, intelligent, lovable, clever, and gay – probably because she had lived so much in society; and also spent time in Munich.

SP: And the Mozarts are well-known for their sharp tongues, of course, and this was something you and Maria shared.

WAM: We exactly suited each other, yes, for like me, she was rather inclined to be satirical, so we bantered as friends most merrily together.

SP: And was your affection for her the reason you turned on Father Emilian?

WAM: Father Emilian?

SP: Father Emilian.

WAM: Father Emilian was a conceited jackass and an idiot, and yes, he was also rather sweet on my cousin, and wished to have his jest with her – but she made a jest of him.

SP: Sounds interesting. What happened?

WAM: Well, we were all rather tipsy, I grant you, and he began to talk about music, and sang a canon, saying, 'I never in my life heard anything finer.'

SP: But you didn't concur?

WAM: I said, 'I regret that I can't sing it with you, for nature has not given me the power of intoning.' 'No matter,' said he. So he began again, and in fact I harmonized with him – but sang different words!

SP: What sort of words?

WAM: Words like 'Pater Emilian, oh! thou numskull', *sotto*

voce to my cousin; then we laughed on for at least half an hour.

SP: And Emilian didn't notice?

WAM: Not at all. He said to me 'If we could only be longer together, we could discuss the art of musical composition!' 'In that case,' said I, 'our discussion would be brief indeed.' A famous rap on the knuckles for him!

SP: But your father disapproved of your relationship with Maria.

WAM: The bitter way in which he wrote about my merry and entirely innocent exchanges with his brother's daughter made me justly indignant, I think, for it was not as he thought, and so I didn't feel obliged to give him an answer on the subject.

SP: No. But you didn't spare women from your sharp tongue. I think of Josepha, who was in love with you.

WAM: Josepha? She was heavy like a peasant wench, her sweat made you sick, and she walked around so scantily clad that, well, one could read the message quite plainly. People genuinely wondered why I would take someone with a face like hers.

SP: But as we've heard, you thought rather differently about Aloysia Weber. Indeed, in your head you were almost married, and you protected her as a husband might.

WAM: There was a grand court concert where poor Mademoiselle Weber felt the fangs of her enemies, for on one occasion she was not asked to sing!

sP: Why was that?

waM: Those Italian scoundrels, the singers of Munich, those infamous charlatans, had circulated a report that she had very much 'fallen off' in her singing.

sP: But it wasn't true?

waM: When Cannabich heard her singing a while after, he said to her, 'Mademoiselle, I hope you will continue to 'fall off' in this manner.'

There is little doubt that Madame Weber encouraged her daughter to flirt with Wolfgang. After all, it would have been a social step up to become a Mozart, which of course is the reason why Leopold Mozart so disapproved of the match. He saw the Weber clan as loose-living and socially beneath them.

Mozart, however, was captivated by the sixteen-year-old, and arrived back in Munich from Paris hopeful of a relationship – only to discover that Aloysia had changed. She did not share his feelings, if indeed she ever had. As she remarked to me: 'I did not know, you see. I only thought he was such a little man.'

Wolfgang's handwriting at this time betrays great agitation of the mind, and Nissen later told me exactly what happened: "Mozart, being in mourning for his mother, appeared dressed, according to the French custom, in a red coat with black buttons; but soon discovered that Aloysia's feelings towards him had undergone a change. She seemed scarcely to recognize the man for whose sake she had once shed so many tears. At which point Mozart quickly seated himself at the piano and sang, 'I gladly give up the girl who slights me.'

SP: Discovering Aloysia no longer had feelings for you was a great shock; the end of a dream.

WAM: I do not wish to give up dreaming, for what mortal on the whole compass of the earth does not often dream?

SP: So what did your dreams look like?

WAM: Above all, dreams of pleasure, peaceful dreams, sweet, cheering dreams if you will, dreams which, if realized, would have rendered my life – more sad than pleasurable in those days – a good deal more endurable.

SP: Certainly your letters at that time reveal a disturbed hand.

WAM: I naturally write very badly, for I never learned to write; still, in my whole life I never wrote worse than that very day, for I really was unfit for anything, my heart was too full of tears.

SP: We'll return to Aloysia, because your paths did cross again – but another woman, Madame Cannabich, became a good friend also.

WAM: Yes, I can safely say that she is one of my best and truest friends, for I only call friends those who are friends in every situation; who, day and night, think how they can best serve the interests of their friend, applying to all influential persons, and toiling to secure their happiness.

SP: In other words, you like your friends to help you find work!

WAM: There may indeed be a strain of self-interest in this, for

where does anything take place – indeed, how can anything
be done in this world – without some alloy of selfishness? But
what I liked best in Madame Cannabich is – and she never
attempts to deny this – that when we were alone, which, I
regret to say, was very seldom, we became quite confidential.

sp: Really?

wam: Oh yes. Of all the intimate friends who frequented
her house, I alone possessed her entire confidence; for I alone
knew all her domestic and family troubles, concerns, secrets,
and circumstances.

sp: But you didn't get on so well on first acquaintance.

wam: We were not nearly so well acquainted the first time I
was there, no – we have agreed on this point. And nor did we
understand each other so well; but living in the same house
affords greater opportunities to know a person.

sp: Quite.

NINE

Mozart's Monsters

Mozart fell out with so many people along the way, that we'll have to be selective as we consider some of Mozart's least favourite folk, who might also be known as Mozart's Monsters.

SP: We've mentioned Becke already. A man you didn't have much time for.

WAM: I care very little about him.

SP: Any particular reason?

WAM: We conversed on a variety of topics – among others, about Vienna, and more particularly about the Emperor Joseph II who, believe me, was no great lover of music.

SP: So where was the problem?

WAM: Becke said, 'When I was to play before the Emperor, I had no idea what to play; so I began with some fugues and trifles of that kind, which in my own mind I only laughed at.' And I, of course, could scarcely resist replying, 'I would have laughed too – but not half so loud as I would have done had I heard you!'

SP: Yes, not one of your friendlier remarks.

WAM: Becke further said, and it's true, that the music in the Emperor's private apartments is enough to frighten the crows. So I replied that whenever I heard such music, if I did not quickly leave the room it gave me a headache. 'Oh no!' he says.

'It has no such effect on me; bad music does not affect my nerves, but fine music never fails to give me a headache.' And I thought to myself: 'such a shallow head as yours is sure to suffer when listening to what is beyond its comprehension!'

SP: And then of course you famously fell out with Langemantl's son, after a night of merriment turned sour.

WAM: We were all very merry, yes. When we came back from the theatre, I played till we went to supper. Young Langenmantl had already questioned me that morning about my cross.

SP: Ah yes – at the age of 14, the Pope conferred on you the Order of the Spur.

WAM: Well, I told him exactly how I got it, and what it was, and then he and his brother-in-law said over and over again, 'Let us order a cross, too, that we may be on a par with Herr Mozart.' They also repeatedly said, 'Hello, thou Sir! Knight of the Spur!'

SP: How did you react?

WAM: I said not a word; but during supper it became really too bad. 'What may it have cost – three ducats? Do you require permission to wear it? Do you pay extra for permission to do so? We really must get one just like it!' And then an officer there said, 'For shame! What would you do with the cross?' and that young ass, Kurzen Mantl, winked at him, but I saw him, and he knew that I did.

SP: The evening was turning nasty.

WAM: Well, a pause ensued, and then Langemantl offered me snuff, saying, 'There, show that you don't care a pinch of snuff for it!' I still said nothing.

SP: You weren't really dealing with it, were you?

WAM: And at length he began once more in a sneering tone: 'Be so good as to lend me the cross for a few minutes, and I will return it immediately after I have spoken to the goldsmith about it, for it's not gold, only copper, ha! ha!' and I said, 'By no means – it is lead, ha! ha!'

SP: You were finally squaring up to the bullies?

WAM: Oh, I was I was burning with anger and rage, and after further deeply unpleasant exchanges, I took my hat and my sword, and said, 'I hope to have the pleasure of seeing you tomorrow.' 'Tomorrow I shall not be here,' he said. 'Well, then, the next morning, when I shall still be here. You are a set of boors, so good night,' and off I went.

SP: Was it all resolved?

WAM: Not at all. Papa thought I had lowered myself by my conduct, but I thought anything but that! I was only straightforward, no more. Langemantl was hardly a boy; he was twenty-one and a married man! Can anyone be considered a boy who is married?

SP: And did you see him again?

WAM: I have never gone near him. I left two cards for him the following day and excused myself for not going in, having so many indispensable calls to make.

sp: Well, I'm sure you didn't miss him. He doesn't sound as though he wished you well. And then there's Vogler, perhaps another one of Mozart's Monsters.

wam: When Vogler came back from Italy –

sp: – where he'd been sent by the Elector –

wam: – he entered the church, was immediately appointed Court Chaplain, and promptly composed a Miserere full of false harmony, which the whole world declared detestable.

sp: That must have been hard for him to take?

wam: Well, hearing that it was not much commended, he went to the Elector and complained that the orchestra played badly on purpose, to vex and annoy him! In short, he knew just how to play the game, entering into so many petty intrigues with women, that eventually he became Vice-Kapellmeister.

sp: A post you might have liked. Though Vogler was the teacher of Karl Maria von Weber, who esteemed him highly. Your criticism seems a little severe.

wam: That man is a fool, who fancies that no one can be better or more perfect than himself, and as I say, the whole orchestra, from the first to the last, detested him.

sp: And of course he's written a book on the art of composing, which I was thinking of buying.

wam: His book is more fit to teach arithmetic than composition. He says that he can make a composer in three weeks, and a singer in six months.

SP: And can he?

WAM: Let us just say that we have not yet seen any proof of this.

SP: Point taken, and so let's move on to Baron Grimm who had been a family friend, but in your head, he became another Mozart Monster when you stayed with him in Paris.

WAM: And do not imagine that he was the same as he used to be –

SP: – when you knew him as a child. Or had you changed perhaps?

WAM: Were it not for Madame d'Epinay, I would not have stayed.

SP: I understand he thought he was being kind to you, providing refuge for a young man far from home.

WAM: Well, he had no cause to be proud of his good deeds towards me, for there were four other houses where I could have had both board and lodging. In fact, if I had remained in Paris, I intended to leave him to go to a house that, unlike his, was neither stupid nor tiresome, and where a man didn't have constantly thrown in his face what a magnificent kindness had been done to him!

SP: So you didn't regret leaving?

WAM: I regretted not remaining with Baron Grimm for one

reason only: because I should have liked to show him that I did not require him, and that I could do quite as much as his beloved Piccini, even though I was a mere German!

SP: And you blamed him for the terrible journey from Paris to Munich which then followed.

WAM: Only because Herr Grimm deceived me! He said I'd arrive at Strasbourg in five days; and I did not find out till the last day that I was in another carriage, which went at a snail's pace, never changed horses, and was ten days on the journey.

SP: Ten days?!

WAM: Ten days! You may easily conceive my rage; but I only gave way to it when with my intimate friends, for in his presence I affected to be quite merry and pleased.

SP: Though you weren't.

WAM: I submitted to this transport for eight days, but longer than that, I couldn't stand, and not on account of discomfort – for the carriage was well-appointed – but from sheer want of sleep. We were off every morning at four o'clock, and thus obliged to rise at three. Twice I had the pleasure of being forced to get up at one o'clock in the morning, as we were to set off at two! I cannot sleep in a moving carriage, so I really could not continue like this without the risk of being ill.

SP: So a thumbs-down to Baron Grimm. But perhaps your top monster of all – well, undoubtedly the top monster – was the Archbishop of Salzburg, Heironymous Colloredo, who both your father and yourself worked for.

WAM: The Archbishop prevented us from earning a living, and yet never paid an equivalent. If he did not allow me to gain my own livelihood –

SP: – by doing concerts and the like –

WAM: – he might at least supply me with money, for I could not live on my own means.

SP: But it wasn't just the money; it was the status as well. In the Archbishop's household in Vienna, you sat with the valets and cooks?

WAM: Herr Von Kleinmaryn and Bonike had a table set apart with the illustrious Count Arco. It would have been a mark of distinction if I were at that table.

SP: Indeed. But were the valets at least good company?

WAM: At table, all kinds of coarse and silly joking went on. But no one joked with me, for I never said a word, or if I was obliged to speak, I did so with the utmost gravity, and then when I was done, I went away. My chief object in the Palace was to find an appropriate way into the presence of the Emperor, for I was quite resolved that he at least should know me.

SP: And then what?

WAM: It would be a great pleasure to play my opera to him, and then some fugues perhaps, for they were his favourites.

SP: And those charity performances in Vienna, when musicians give their time and skill freely. Did you take part in those?

WAM: No.

SP: Why not?

WAM: The Archbishop would not permit it.

SP: But it's charity work!

WAM: He would not permit me do it, and yes, all the nobility took my absence highly amiss.

SP: And yet the Archbishop wouldn't let you play for personal gain either?

WAM: If I were to have given a concert, the sum I would have made! But no, our Archbishop did not want people to have any profit – only loss.

SP: And in the end, your patience gave way, and you decided to leave his service.

WAM: I was filled with the gall of bitterness, and yes, my long-tried patience at last gave way.

SP: So what happened?

WAM: The Archbishop said the most insulting things to my face.

SP: What sort of things?

WAM: He called me a knave, a dissolute fellow, and I was

twice called a coward.

SP: That all sounds quite insulting. And your reaction?

WAM: I was silent, as my father would have it.

SP: And in Vienna at that time, you didn't feel alone. The Archbishop was attacking you, but you felt surrounded by friends.

WAM: I had the best and most useful acquaintances in the world, who treated me with every possible consideration.

SP: Though you were worried that your father, still employed by the Archbishop, might reap the backlash of any clash between the two of you.

WAM: If I had not been afraid of perhaps harming him, I would have acted much sooner in this matter. But really, what could the Archbishop do to him? Nothing!

SP: Though his insults hurt you.

WAM: Oh yes! It had such an effect on my bodily frame that the same evening at the opera I was obliged to go home in the middle of the first act and lie down, for I was feverish, trembled in every limb – and staggered down the street like a drunken man.

SP: So just what was the Archbishop upset about?

WAM: He called me a ragamuffin, a scamp, a rogue!

SP: Yes – but why?

WAM: I will tell you the chief reproach against my service: I did not know that I was a valet, and this was my ruin!

SP: How do you mean?

WAM: Apparently, I ought to have loitered every morning for a couple of hours in the anteroom. I was told that I should show myself more, but somehow I could never understand why it was part of my duty – so I only came punctually when the Archbishop summoned me.

SP: And how did your father respond to this affair?

WAM: With a burst of anger.

SP: Just when you needed his support.

WAM: I implored him to strengthen me in my resolution, rather than trying to dissuade me, for it only made me miserable and idle. After all, my wish and hope was to gain honour, fame, and money; and I had every confidence that I could be more useful to him in Vienna than Salzburg.

SP: But your father was intransigent, and wrote harshly.

WAM: I confess I did not recognize my father in these letters!

SP: It was that bad?

WAM: A father indeed, but not a kind, loving father, concerned for the honour of his children and his own – in short, not *my* father.

SP: What did he say?

WAM: He said I had never shown any love for him, and therefore ought to show it on this occasion. Could he really be saying this?

SP: It's not out of character. And he also accused you of being interested only in pleasure.

WAM: Huh! If pleasure means having got away from a prince who paid me badly and constantly bullied me, then it's true that my pleasure was great! I was forced to take this step and would never deviate from it by a single hair's breadth!

SP: No turning back?

WAM: Impossible!

SP: And to add to your grief, your father thought you were a spendthrift.

WAM: Well, I certainly am no miser, as it would be difficult for me to be stingy. Yet the people here consider me more disposed to be a niggard than a spendthrift!

SP: I suppose your father was thinking back to Munich.

WAM: Ah, well it is true that in Munich I stupidly showed myself to him in a false light, for I had too much amusement there, yes. But my merriment was only youthful folly, for goodness sake! I thought to myself: where am I going next? To Salzburg! So until then, let me enjoy myself!

SP: Salzburg felt like death.

WAM: I admit I longed for a hundred amusements in

Salzburg, but in Vienna, not one. To be in Vienna was pleasure enough. I was no longer a fool; nor was I a godless or ungrateful son. And as for the Archbishop, I was more highly prized in Vienna than he was.

sp: Really?

wam: He was known only as an arrogant, presumptuous priest, despising everyone, whereas I was considered an obliging person.

sp: An obliging person maybe, yet in his letters, your father always took the Archbishop's side.

wam: His letters only served to irritate my mind, and to disturb my head and spirit, and as I was constantly occupied in composing, I required both a cheerful mind and a heart at rest.

sp: And you never got on with the Archbishop's sidekick, Count Arco.

wam: No.

sp: Not helped by your father actually writing to *him*, to complain about your conduct.

wam: Indeed.

sp: So what did you say to the Count when he raised the matter?

wam: I interrupted him –

SP: Interrupted him?

WAM: I interrupted him saying, 'My father has also written to *me,* and in such a manner, frankly, that I thought it would drive me crazy!'

SP: And Count Arco's attitude?

WAM: 'Believe me, Mozart' he said 'you allow yourself to be too easily dazzled. A man's fame here in Vienna is of a very short duration. After some months have elapsed, the Viennese will want something new.'

SP: And he also said the Archbishop viewed you as a rather 'self-sufficient' young man.

WAM: 'I dare say he does,' I said, 'for I am so towards him. Just as people behave towards me, so I behave towards them. When I see a person despises me and treats me with contempt, I can be as proud as any peacock.'

SP: And did you believe the Count? I mean, did you believe that the Viennese would tire of you?

WAM: This was certainly pianoforte land. And even supposing they did tire of me, it wouldn't be the case for some years. By that time, I reckoned I'd have gained both renown and money.

SP: In the meantime, however, you were literally kicked out of service by the count. He kicked you on the backside?!

WAM: The clown and saucy fellow – turned me out of the room with a kick, yes. Oh, but I forget – that was probably an archiepiscopal command.

sp: Did you dream of revenge?

wam: I knew my practical reply would not fail that jackass, even it were twenty years hence; unless of course, I was unlucky enough to encounter him in some sacred place.

sp: Run for the sanctuary, Count Arco – Mozart's coming!

wam: If anyone offends me, I must have my revenge – though really, I am too proud to measure myself with that stupid oaf.

sp: Yet still your father blamed you for this fall out. He heard stories about you boasting that you ate meat on a fast day.

wam: It is simply not true.

sp: Not true at all?

wam: Simply not true. I did not boast I ate meat on fast days; though I did say I cared little about it, and considered it no sin.

sp: I suppose that could sound like boasting.

wam: But I attended Mass every Sunday, and rest assured, I certainly have a real sense of religion.

sp: Oh I'm sure, I'm sure –

wam: All Vienna knows that this business with the Archbishop occurred because of my injured honor. So what am I to do – proclaim myself a cur and the Archbishop a noble prince? No man could do the former, least of all I; and as for the latter, well, that can only be done by God should He choose to enlighten the prelate!

SP: So you've encountered a fair few monsters, Wolfgang.
What about friends?

WAM: You know well that the best and truest of all friends are
the poor.

SP: Really?

WAM: Oh yes. The rich know nothing of friendship, especially
those who are born to riches; though even those whom *fate*
enriches often become very different when fortunate in life.

SP: New money doesn't make new people.

WAM: No – but when a man is placed in favourable
circumstances, not by blind luck but by reasonable good
fortune and merit, who during his early and less prosperous
days never lost courage, remaining faithful to his religion and
his God, and strove always to be an honest man and good
Christian, knowing how to value his true friends – in short,
one who really deserves better fortune.

SP: Not unlike yourself, Wolfgang.

WAM: From such a man no ingratitude is to be feared.

TEN

The art of criticism

SP: I'm taking you back in time, Wolfgang. It's July 1782, and your opera *The Abduction From the Harem* is a great success – indeed your greatest stage success outside Vienna. But somehow, your father can't find it in him to celebrate. He just reminds you that 'the world' says you'd made an enemy of all professors of music by your boastings and criticism.

WAM: The world? What world? Probably the Salzburg world, for people in Vienna could not fail to see the exact opposite.

SP: But let's reflect for a moment on Mozart the music critic, because you did like to have your say.

WAM: I tell you, I once heard a mass in Mannheim, where it was the custom for the organist to play during the whole of the Benedictus. I heard the second organist first, and then the other.

SP: Which was better?

WAM: In my opinion the second was preferable to the first; for when I heard the former, I asked, 'Who is that playing on the organ?' 'Our second organist,' I was told. 'He plays miserably,' I said. Then the other began, and I said, 'Who's that?' 'Our first organist,' came the reply. 'Amazing,' I said, 'he plays more miserably still!'

SP: You can be a harsh critic.

WAM: Really, it was enough to kill one with laughing to look at those gentlemen.

sp: Not everyone can be as good as you.

wam: The second at the organ was like a child trying to lift a millstone. No really – you could see the anguish in his face! The first wore spectacles, and I stood beside him at the organ and watched him with the intention of learning something from him.

sp: Really?

wam: At each note he lifted his hands entirely off the keys, and often chose to dispense altogether with his right hand when there was not the slightest need to do so, playing with the left alone. In short, he fancied that he could do as he willed, a thorough master of his organ.

sp: But you begged to differ.

wam: As I say, it was enough to kill oneself laughing to look at those gentlemen.

sp: And not all opera singers gave you pleasure either.

wam: Herr Raaff, an old but renowned tenor –

sp: – you've mentioned him –

wam: – he sang in a manner which gave rise to the remark that 'his want of voice was the principal cause of his singing so badly'.

sp: True, possibly; cruel certainly.

WAM: When he began an air, I defied anyone not to burst out laughing. Certainly for myself, if I had not known that this was the celebrated tenor Raaff, I should have been bent double from laughing. As it was, I merely took out my handkerchief to hide a smile.

SP: But was he at least a good actor?

WAM: They tell me here that he was never a good actor; that people went to hear, but not to see him. Though I remember in one opera when he was to die, he sang a long, slow air.

SP: And?

WAM: Well, towards the end of the aria, his voice failed him so entirely that it was impossible to bear it! I was in the orchestra at the time, next to Wendling the flute player. He'd previously criticized the song, saying it was unnatural for anyone to sing so long before dying, adding, 'Maybe he'll never die!' So I said in return, 'Have a little patience, Wendling; soon it'll all be over, for I can definitely hear he's at his last gasp!' 'And I too!' said Wendling, laughing.

SP: And of course you have no time for Vogler or his compositions.

WAM: Hear this: I was once present at a rehearsal of his, but came away immediately after the Kyrie. Never in my life had I heard anything like it.

SP: What was wrong?

WAM: There was endless false harmony, and he rambled into different keys, as if he wished to drag you into them by the hair of your head! Really, I shall say nothing of the way in which he carries out his ideas.

SP: Oh go on.

WAM: Well, I say only that no Mass of Vogler's could possibly please any composer.

SP: Why not?

WAM: I suddenly hear an idea which is not bad.

SP: And then?

WAM: Well, instead of remaining not bad, I imagine it might soon become good?

SP: And does it?

WAM: Not at all! It becomes not only bad, but very bad, and this in various ways: for instance, scarcely has the theme arisen when something else interferes to destroy it; or, it doesn't remain good because he does not finish it naturally; or again, the theme is not introduced in the right place; or it is just ruined by poor instrumentation.

SP: I think we'll take that as a 'Could do better'. But as a critic, do you like difficult music?

WAM: You know that I am no lover of mere difficulties.

SP: Franzl plays difficult music sometimes.

WAM: He plays difficult music, but it does not appear to be so;

indeed, it seems as if one could easily do the same, and this is real talent. It is far easier, you see, to play a thing quickly than slowly.

sp: Really?

wam: Oh yes, if you play quickly, some notes may then be dropped without being observed. But is this genuine music? In rapid playing, the right and left hands may be changed, and no one either sees or hears it – but is this good? The skill, surely, is to play the piece in the time in which it ought to be played, and to express all the notes with proper taste and feeling as written; so that it gives the impression of being composed by the person who plays it.

sp: So you don't like speed for speed's sake. And neither are you a fan of the operatic wobble.

wam: Meissner, as you know, had the bad habit of purposely making his voice tremble at times – entire quavers and even crotchets, when marked 'sustain' – and this I never could endure in him. Nothing can be more truly odious; besides, it's a style of singing quite contrary to nature.

sp: How do you mean?

wam: Well, the human voice is naturally tremulous, but only so far as to be beautiful. Such is the nature of the voice, and it's imitated not only on wind instruments, but on stringed instruments, and even on the piano. But the moment the proper boundary is passed, it is no longer beautiful, because it becomes unnatural, and sounds to me just like an organ when the bellows are panting. Now Raaff, to his credit, never does this; in fact, he cannot bear it.

SP: Ah, Herr Raaff is redeemed! It's good to end on a positive note.

ELEVEN

Performance art

*Mozart began lessons at the age of four with his violinist father.
He was composing from the age of five, and at the age of six he
was mesmerizing European royalty, as he and his gifted sister
Nannerl undertook concert tours across the continent. He played
whatever instrument was at hand – harpsichord at first, the piano
increasingly, and the organ. He was also a very good violinist.*

SP: And of course Wolfgang, you have always been, and
remain, a great performer.

WAM: I remember I played with the Emperor in attendance.
I was encored in the rondo, so when I again seated myself at
the piano, instead of repeating the rondo, I had the music desk
removed and played extemporary.

SP: Is that called showing off?

WAM: You should have seen how this little surprise delighted
the public! They not only applauded vehemently but shouted
'Bravo!' and 'Bravissimo!'

SP: And the Emperor?

WAM: The Emperor listened to me to the end, and when I left
the piano, he left his box – so he'd evidently remained only to
hear me.

SP: And did concerts tire you?

WAM: After three subscription concerts and one in a theatre, towards the end, yes, I was quite worn out by incessant playing, and I think it is much to my credit that my audience was not in a similar state!

s p : And people love *watching* you play as well as listening.

wa m : I remember one man looked steadily at my fingers when I was playing to him, and then suddenly exclaimed: 'Good heavens! How do I labour and overheat myself without getting any applause, while to you, my dear friend, it all seems like child's play!'

s p : And how did you reply?

wa m : I replied, 'Believe me, I once took trouble enough so that one day I would not need to.'

s p : And that reminds me of the concert pianist who came off stage, to be confronted by an admirer who said, 'You're so lucky to be able to play like that!' To which they replied, 'Yes, eight-hours-practice-a-day lucky.' So tell me, because people often ask: who makes the best pianos?

wa m : Spath's pianos were my favourites once; but now I must give preference to those of Stein, for they damp much better than those in Ratisbon. If I strike hard, for instance, whether I let my fingers rest on the notes or lift them, the tone dies away at the same instant that it is heard. So however I strike the keys, the tone always remains even, neither jarring nor failing to sound.

s p : Are Herr Stein's pianos expensive?

wa m : A piano of this kind is not to be had for less than three hundred florins, but the pains and skill which Stein bestows on them cannot be sufficiently repaid.

SP: With pianos, you get what you pay for.

WAM: When he's completed an instrument of this class, he tries all kinds of passages and runs on it, and works away at it, testing its powers till it's capable of doing anything, for he labours not for his own benefit alone – or he might save himself much trouble – but for that of music.

SP: He's a musician before he's a businessman.

WAM: Indeed, he often says, 'If I were not such a passionate lover of music, Wolfgang, playing a little on the piano myself, I should long ago have lost patience with my work – but I like my instruments to respond to the player, and to be durable.'

SP: And are they durable?

WAM: Oh yes, his pianos really do last well. He warrants the sounding board neither breaking nor cracking; for when he has finished one, he exposes it in the air to rain, snow, sun, and every kind of devilry, that it may give way, and then he inserts slips of wood which he glues in, making it quite strong and solid.

SP: He wants it to crack?

WAM: Oh yes, he is actually very glad when it *does* crack, for then he is pretty sure nothing further can happen to it!

SP: So he produces wonderful pianos. But of course you like the organ too.

WAM: When I said to Herr Stein that I should like to play on one of his organs, as the organ was my passion, he seemed surprised, and said, 'What? So great a pianist as you would like to play on an instrument devoid of sweetness and expression, with no gradations from *piano* to *forte*, but always sounding the same?'

SP: My thoughts exactly.

WAM: 'To me that signifies nothing,' I said. 'The organ always was, both in my eyes and ears, the king of all instruments.' 'Well, just as you please,' he said. So we went together, and I could tell from his conversation that he did not expect me to do great things on his organ, presumably thinking that I should handle it in the style of a piano.

SP: The two being very different?

WAM: Indeed, so when we came to the organ loft, I began a prelude, and he just laughed. A fugue followed. 'I can now quite understand why you like to play the organ,' he said, 'when you can play in that manner.'

SP: But is it hard playing someone else's instrument – one you are not familiar with – because I suppose each piano and organ has its own peculiar ways?

WAM: At first the pedal on this organ was a little awkward for me, as it was without the breaks, beginning with C, then D and E in one row, whereas with us D and E are above, just where E flat and F sharp are – but I quickly mastered it.

SP: And you and the organ also caused quite a stir at the Monastery of the Holy Cross.

WAM: A small clavichord was brought in, on which I played a prelude, and then a sonata and the Fischer variations.

SP: They liked it?

WAM: And then some of those present whispered to the Dean that he ought to hear me play in the organ style. I asked him to give me a theme, which he declined, but one of the monks did.

SP: God bless him.

WAM: I handled it quite calmly at first, and then suddenly, the fugue being in G minor, I introduced a lively movement in the major key, but in the same tempo – and then again at the end of the original subject, only reversed.

SP: You were enjoying yourself.

WAM: And of course then it occurred to me to employ the lively movement for the subject of the fugue also, and did so at once –

SP: You were improvising?

WAM: And it all went as accurate as if a Salzburg tailor had taken its measure!

SP: Providing almost indecent thrills in the monastery.

WAM: Well yes, the Dean was in a state of great excitement. 'It's done,' he said, 'and it's no use talking about it, but I can scarcely believe what I have just heard. Mind you, my prelate did tell me that in his life, he'd never heard anyone play the organ in a more finished and solid style!'

SP: You were getting more praise than God.

WAM: And then someone brought me a fugued sonata, and asked me to play it. But I said, 'Gentlemen, I really must suggest that this is asking rather too much, for it's hardly likely that I'll be able to play such a sonata at sight.' 'Indeed, I think so too,' said the Dean eagerly, wishing to favour me, 'it is too much; no one could do it.' 'At all events,' I said 'I suppose I can but *try*.' I heard the Dean muttering all the time behind me, 'Oh, you rogue! Oh, you knave!'

SP: You played it.

WAM: I played till 11 o'clock, quite bombarded and besieged by fugue themes.

SP: You did get around, didn't you?

WAM: I was in Munich once, on the stately and solemn occasion of the name day of his Royal Highness the Archduke Albert.

SP: Very grand.

WAM: We had a select music party at home, which started at half past three and finished at eight. Monsieur Dubreuil, whom papa knew, was also present; he was a pupil of Tartini.

SP: A good pupil?

WAM: Well, first of all we played the two quintets of Haydn, but to my dismay I could scarcely hear Dubreuil, who could not play four continuous bars without a mistake. He could never find the positions, and he was no friend to the short pause either!

sp: Not the ideal partner.

wam: The only good thing was that he spoke politely and praised the quintets. But apart from that, I said nothing, though he kept constantly saying to himself, 'Oh, I beg your pardon, but I'm out of time again! The thing is puzzling – but fine!'

sp: Were you patient with him?

wam: Oh yes. I invariably replied, 'It's of no consequence, Dubreuil; after all, we are only among ourselves.' I then played the concertos in C, in B, and in E flat, and after that a trio of mine. In the adagio, however, I was obliged to play six bars of his part as well.

sp: Which I'm sure you managed with ease.

wam: And as a finale, I played my last divertimento in B; and then how they pricked up their ears! I played as if I had been the greatest violin player in all Europe.

sp: And the greatest piano player in all Europe?

wam: Well, I was told that when Misliweczeck heard people here speaking of Becke, or indeed other performers on the piano, he invariably said, 'Let no one deceive himself; none can play like Mozart; in Italy, where the greatest masters are, they speak of no one but Mozart. When his name is mentioned, not a word is said of others.'

TWELVE

Vienna

The Archbishop of Salzburg, Wolfgang's nemesis, uprooted to Vienna in 1781. He was keen to appear in the Imperial city in the full splendour of a spiritual prince, and so took with him – in addition to fine furniture and a large household – some of his most distinguished musicians, one of them being Mozart. It was a defining moment in the wandering Wolfgang's life – he would never again live anywhere but Vienna.

At first, it was a match made in heaven. Vienna loved his touch and improvisation, and he earned money from selling compositions, performing, and teaching. It was in Vienna he got married; acquired a billiard table and a horse; became a mason; and wrote the operas Don Giovanni, The Marriage of Figaro, The Magic Flute *and his unfinished* Requiem.

WAM: Germans are people who have always excelled the most in fine arts.

SP: Indeed. But they've had to go abroad to be appreciated. I think of the 'London Bach' for instance and Handel, who both settled in England. And you too have thought of such a move once or twice.

WAM: If Germany, my beloved fatherland, would not accept me, then yes, in God's name let France or England be enriched by one more German talent – to the disgrace of the German nation.

SP: And on that international theme, I was surprised to find you so pleased with the recent military outcomes at Gibraltar, when the English repelled the Spanish attack.

WA M: I did hear of that with the greatest joy, yes, for you
know I'm thoroughly English at heart.

SP: You haven't forgotten your stay in London?

WA M: I have now taken some English lessons, and I hope in
the course of three months to be able to read and understand
English books very tolerably.

SP: But you didn't write *Don Giovanni* for the English; you
wrote it for the Bohemians.

WA M: *Don Giovanni* was written for the people of Prague, yes,
but most of all for me and my friends.

SP: Why Prague?

WA M: The Bohemians are the ones who understand me.

SP: *The Marriage of Figaro* went down very well there. But you
stayed in Vienna?

WA M: Oh, I assure you Vienna is a splendid place, and for my
profession, the best place in the world. I like being here, but
of course I strive to derive benefit from it also. Believe me, my
sole purpose is to make as much money as possible, which next
to health, is best of all.

SP: Wealth and health. And applause?

WA M: What delights and surprises me most of all is both
the extraordinary silence and the cries of 'bravo' while I am

playing. This is certainly honour enough in Vienna, where there are so many good pianists.

SP: But it was a big move. Did you feel you were losing touch with your father back in Salzburg; or was your father losing touch with you?

WAM: I begged him never to allow the thought to cross his mind that I could ever forget him, for I could not bear such an idea. My chief aim was, and always would be, to work so that we could meet soon and happily. But patience was necessary. We know that things often take a perverse turn, I said, but they will one day go straight – only patience!

SP: Perhaps harder for your father than for you.

WAM: I said to my father that I placed faith in three friends – and that they are powerful and invincible ones!

SP: And who were these three friends?

WAM: God, his head, and mine.

SP: But you were very different men.

WAM: Oh yes, our heads were very different, but each in its own way was good, serviceable, and useful. I told him to remember he had a son who never intentionally failed in his filial duty towards him, and who would strive to become daily more worthy of so good a father.

SP: But even though he was in Salzburg and you here in Vienna, he still advised you about everything – even house-hunting. He wanted you to stay with Herr Aurnhammer, and you did visit. Was it nice?

WAM: Nice for rats and mice, but not for human beings.

SP: You didn't like it. I remember you saying it was a bit gloomy.

WAM: Believe me – a lantern was required to light me upstairs at *noon*.

SP: And your room?

WAM: The room might be called a closet and to get to it, I had to pass through the kitchen, and then above my door was a small window.

SP: So?

WAM: They promised to put up a curtain, whilst requesting me to open it as soon as I'd dressed – otherwise, they could not see at all, either in the kitchen or adjoining room!

SP: Yes, that's not ideal.

WAM: All in all, it was miserable to behold, and his wife, the most stupid, gossiping woman imaginable. Basta! No more!

SP: And really, they wanted you for your name.

WAM: Worthy people, yes, who had sufficient shrewdness to see how useful my acquaintance was to their daughter, who, incidentally, was the most tiresome creature I ever knew.

SP: Apart, of course, from the daughter of Frau Adlgasserin, who was rather – how shall we say? – fond of you.

WAM: She was seriously smitten with me, yes.

SP: And you with her?

WAM: No! Indeed, if a painter wished to depict the devil according to nature, he could not do better than have recourse to her face.

SP: You taught her the piano.

WAM: I told her the truth in a civil manner, but it did no good and she became more loving than ever. 'Dear Mozart,' she said, 'don't be so cross. You may say what you please but I shall always like you.'

SP: And behind your back, people were saying you two were to marry.

WAM: Yes, and she would confirm it! Basta! She was nothing but an amorous fool.

SP: And of course you struggled to dress well enough for Vienna

WAM: No house-painter has shirts as coarse as mine, which is certainly the most unseemly thing of all in a man.

SP: You think?

WAM: Clothes are a constant expense. The grand principle here in Vienna is not to make yourself too cheap, for that is utter ruin.

SP: You must dress to impress?

WAM: The most pretentious always obtain preference here.

SP: I'll remember that. But in the meantime, what was a day like in those early years in Vienna?

WAM: Every morning at six o'clock my hairdresser would wake me.

SP: Yes, I met him. He'd curl, dress, and powder your hair, because a certain artificiality of appearance does seem to be the height of fashion here.

WAM: I'd have finished dressing by seven, and then I'd write till ten. I'd then give a lesson to Frau Von Trattner. At eleven, I'd go to Countess Rumbeck and I'd go every day, unless they sent to put me off, which annoyed me.

SP: I can understand that.

WAM: I'd dine at one o'clock, unless I was invited out. If I was, then I could not begin to work again until five or six, though I was often prevented from this by some concert. Otherwise, I'd write till nine.

SP: A long day.

WAM: And not over, for then I'd go to my dear Constanze –

SP: Ah yes, your then wife-to-be!

WAM: Though our pleasure in meeting was frequently embittered by the unkind rantings of her mother – hence my desire to rescue her as soon as possible.

s P: And then?

wa M: At half past ten or eleven I'd go home, though that depended on her mother's mood, or my patience in bearing it.

s P: But then it was definitely time for bed.

wa M: Yes, though if I was summoned to a concert and got home early, then I'd write until one, and rise again at six.

s P: Fascinating, and it may be a bit gossipy, but I hear Frau Weber liked her wine.

wa M: Yes she did, and perhaps more than a woman ought.

s P: This is what I heard.

wa M: Still, I never saw her at all intoxicated, and it would be false if I were to say so.

s P: Admirable honesty, given you didn't take to her.

wa M: And believe me, the children drank nothing but water, for although she pressed wine upon them, she never succeeded.

s P: You mean she tried to persuade them to drink?

wa M: Oh yes. So often there was great wrangling on the subject. I mean, can anyone conceive a mother quarrelling with her children on such a point?

s P: It's usually the other way round, I agree. And of course it was Constanze who encouraged you to write fugues. How did that come about?

WAM: After I played them to him, Baron Von Swieten would give me all of Handel's and Bach's fugues to take home with me; and when Constanze heard these, she fell in love with them at once.

SP: She was a huge fugue fan.

WAM: She'll listen to nothing but fugues, particularly the work of Handel and Bach, and as she often heard me playing fugues out of my head, she asked me if I ever wrote them down, and when I said I never did, she reproached me for not having composed this most artistic and beautiful style of music – and then never ceased in her entreaties until I wrote a fugue for her!

SP: And then came your opera *The Marriage of Figaro* – a rather savage lampoon of the Viennese propensity for sexual intrigue. Yet while it may have made you enemies here, it seemed to melt your father. He came to visit you and Constanze in Vienna when it was performed, and proudly records that at the second performance there were five encores, and at the third performance, seven encores!

WAM: It was the same reception in Prague. And my goodness, you ought to have been there, all those pretty creatures married and single!

SP: Well, I hope you behaved.

WAM: I neither danced nor flirted with any of them – the former because I was too tired, and the latter from my natural bashfulness. But there, believe me, nothing was talked of but 'Figaro', nothing played but 'Figaro', nothing whistled or sung but 'Figaro', no opera so crowded as 'Figaro' – in short, nothing but 'Figaro'!

SP: Rather flattering, I imagine.

WAM: Very flattering to me, certainly.

SP: And for once, your father took your side instead of your enemies'. He wrote to your sister saying that it would say much for the work if it was successful, 'for I know that very strong cabals have formed against it. Salieri and all his satellites will again move heaven and earth to ensure its failure. Your brother,' he continued, 'is the object of many hostile intrigues entirely due to his remarkable talent and genius gaining him so great a reputation.' So! Praise at last from your father who, like you, became a mason; but also died that year.

WAM: The mournful tidings of the death of my excellent father, yes. You may conceive the state I was in.

SP: Yes, I'm sure, I'm sure. Though by that time, he was back in Salzburg, and you didn't return for the funeral.

WAM: No.

THIRTEEN

Marriage

SP: You were always fascinated by women, but you didn't rush into anything.

WAM: I hoped never to marry for money; I wished to make my wife happy, but not to become rich by her means.

SP: Quite.

WAM: God has not bestowed talents on me to invest them in a rich wife and to waste my time in idleness. I certainly had nothing to say against matrimony in my youth, but it would have been a misfortune to me then.

SP: So you bided your time.

WAM: Yes, I decided to let things alone, and enjoy my golden freedom till I was so well off that I could support both wife and children. Herr Schiedenhofen, for instance, was forced to choose a rich wife; his title imposed this on him.

SP: The nobility are different, I suppose.

WAM: Oh, the nobility must not marry for love or inclination, but from interest, and all kinds of other considerations! It would not at all suit a grandee to love his wife after she had done her duty, and brought into the world an heir to the property. God forbid! But we poor humble people, on the other hand, are privileged to choose a wife who loves us, and whom we love. We need no wealthy wife, for our riches are in our heads, and these no man can deprive us of, unless he cut them off – in which case we need nothing more!

sp: Good point. Though of course there was gossip about you because you stayed with the Webers who had four daughters.

wam: Groundless reports, in which there was not a word of truth.

sp: But you liked Constanze?

wam: I bantered and jested with her when time permitted, but nothing more. If I were obliged to marry all those with whom I jested, I should have at least 200 wives.

sp: But marriage seemed increasingly attractive.

wam: My disposition has always inclined me more towards domestic life than excitement, yes. I never, for instance, from my youth upwards, have been responsible for my linen and clothes, and so I thought nothing more desirable for me than a wife –

sp: – who could handle these things.

wam: An unmarried man, in my opinion, can enjoy only half a life.

sp: But you were now closing in on one of the Weber daughters. Which one, I wonder?

wam: Well, not Josepha who is idle, coarse, and deceitful; crafty and cunning as a fox.

sp: I can see why you avoided her.

WAM: Aloysia, now Madame Lange –

SP: – your previous infatuation –

WAM: – is false and unprincipled, a coquette, while the youngest daughter was still too young to have a character defined. The third, however, namely my good and beloved Constanze, was the martyr of the family, and probably on this account the most kindhearted, cleverest, and best of them all.

SP: She was the one for Wolfgang; your soul's crescendo, your 'bravissimo!'

WAM: She took charge of the whole house, and yet apparently did nothing right in their eyes. Believe me, I have never before encountered such diversity of disposition within one family.

SP: How did she look?

WAM: She was not plain, but at the same time far from being handsome.

SP: I see.

WAM: Her beauty consists in a pair of bright black eyes and a pretty figure. She is not witty –

SP: – there's more to life than comedy –

WAM: – but has enough good sense to enable her to fulfill her duties as a wife and mother. She dresses her own hair, understands housekeeping and has the best heart in the world.

SP: All important in their own way.

WAM: Yes, I love her with my whole soul, as she does me.

SP: But there were problems. Frau Weber wanted to pin you down to your commitment, and her guardian actually made you write a letter of obligation, promising that you would marry Constanze – with serious financial implications if you didn't.

WAM: It was all a misunderstanding.

SP: And then of course your father was angry about this relationship; didn't like it at all. Was he right to be angry?

WAM: He had a right to be displeased, a perfect right. But having read my justification, I did think he might forgive me. And I implored him to give his consent.

SP: Was he withholding it?

WAM: I said I could never be happy and contented without my dear Constanze; and without his satisfied acquiescence, I could only be half happy. Therefore, I said, make me wholly happy!

SP: But he withheld it, to your deep frustration. And then when it finally came, two things strike me. First, it was through gritted teeth, with him almost disowning you. But second, and more interestingly, you'd already gone ahead and got married anyway, the day before it arrived! Amidst all your protestations of parental devotion, you're actually someone who does what you want, Wolfgang, and not what other people want.

WAM: He was a kind and considerate father, to whom I owe everything.

SP: Of course, so moving on, was the marriage a big affair?

WAM: No one attended the wedding apart from Constanze's mother and youngest sister. Herr Von Thorwarth was also there in his capacity as guardian, Herr Von Zetto who gave away the bride, and Gilofsky, my best man.

SP: And how did you feel?

WAM: When the ceremony was over, both my wife and I shed tears.

SP: You were moved.

WAM: All present, even the priest, were touched on seeing the emotions of our hearts! Man and wife are one.

SP: But not man and mother-in-law.

WAM: No, we visited her after our marriage, but on the second visit, quarrelling and wrangling began again, so that my poor wife burst into tears. I put a stop to it at once by saying it was time to go, and we did not go back for a while.

SP: So there was much happiness after the marriage. But it hadn't been all sweet romance with Constanze, leading up to the day. Indeed, you got very angry with her when you heard that in a game of forfeits, her forfeit was to allow her left leg to be measured!

WAM: No girl with becoming modesty would have permitted such a thing.

SP: And after your outburst, Constanze actually broke off the engagement.

WAM: This is true.

SP: Though apparently Baroness Waldstätten did the same; I mean, also had her leg measured as a forfeit.

WAM: If it was true the Baroness did the same, then that was irrelevant, because she was an elderly woman, past it, and someone who could not possibly charm anyone anymore.

SP: And her reputation was a little tarnished, I understand.

WAM: She was always rather flighty, yes, and I hoped Constanze would never lead a life like hers!

SP: Though just for clarity, Wolfgang, is this the same baroness you later refer to as 'dearest, best and fairest; golden, silver and sugared; most perfect and precious, highly esteemed baroness'?

WAM: Well, I have since received much courtesy from her.

SP: I see. And meanwhile Constanze was worried your father wouldn't like her when they met.

WAM: She had a lurking fear.

SP: Hardly surprising.

WAM: And all because she was not pretty, of course, but I did my best to console her by assuring her that my dearest father thought more of inward than outward beauty.

sp: Words which consoled her greatly, no doubt.

As a postscript to this conversation, I record that their nine-year marriage was by all accounts a happy one. As she said to me after his death, 'His letters are the best indicators of how he was thinking, and admirably constant is his extraordinary love for me, which breathes through all his letters. Those of his last year on earth are just as tender as those which he must have written in the first year of our married life. Is it not so?'

I checked the letters, and yes, it was so.

FOURTEEN

Hard times

On his arrival in Vienna, in 1781, Mozart's piano playing found him a niche. But by 1786, his performances were no longer a novelty. Count Arco had been right: Vienna was quick to move on, and fickle in its affections. Emperor Joseph II commissioned the comic opera Così fan Tutte, *performed in January 1790. But Joseph died before hearing it, and without providing for the future of the composer.*

Mozart's last few years in Vienna were spent earning too little and spending too much. Teaching was difficult because the rich disappeared in the summer, and travel to houses was either expensive or time-consuming. He didn't skimp on clothes, however. In 1782, he desired a beautiful red coat, and some buttons which impressed him:

'I simply must have such a jacket so it will be worth my while to get those buttons, which I just can't get out of my mind – mother of pearl with several white stones around the edge and a beautiful yellow stone in the middle.'

Despite his protestations, Wolfgang loved to spend, despite being – as one observer cruelly suggested – a 'working stiff': a musician in a Europe teeming with musicians who were more highly esteemed than him.

SP: Times were so hard last year, Wolfgang, that you were actually composing music for a clock?

WAM: I was firmly resolved to write the Adagio for the clockmaker at once so that I might drop a few ducats into the hands of my dear little wife.

SP: This was music that would play inside the clock on little pipes?

WAM: And I began it, but was unlucky enough – because I hate such work – not to be able to finish it.

SP: The clock was a block?

WAM: I worked at it every day, but had to give up because it bored me.

SP: Yet it was a commission.

WAM: Oh, I hoped to force it through in time. And I mean, if it had been a large clockwork with a sound like an organ, then I'd have been glad to do it. But as the music came from tiny pipes only, well, the sound was just too shrill and childish for me.

SP: It must be hard for a man who's written for orchestras to be reduced to writing for clocks. But as you say, you needed the money. And you were always looking for work. You wanted the musical director job in Vienna.

WAM: I knew for certain that the Emperor intended to establish a German opera in Vienna, and was eagerly looking out for a young musical director who understood the German language, had genius, and was capable of bringing something new into the world.

SP: That's you, Wolfgang.

WAM: Benda applied, but Schweitzer was also determined to succeed. I thought it would be just the thing for me, and well-paid of course. I asked my father to write to every kind friend he could think of in Vienna, saying that I was capable of doing credit to the Emperor.

SP: But you didn't get the post.

WAM: No. I mean, if the Emperor would do nothing else, he could at least try me with an opera, and as to what may occur thereafter, I cared not.

SP: And when people say they don't care, it's a sign that something's snapped; a sign of frustration. Do your father's accusations of being a spendthrift and not valuing money still haunt you?

WAM: How could I have learned to value money? I never had enough of it in my hands! I remember that once when I had 20 ducats I thought myself rich. Need alone teaches the value of money.

SP: And so you moved out of the city centre, to where we now sit, to save money?

WAM: I thought the apartment quite as good, if not better, for I didn't have much to do in town, wouldn't be exposed to so many visits and could therefore work harder.

SP: It's a nice place.

WAM: And not only cheaper but far more agreeable in spring, summer and autumn, especially as here I have a garden.

SP: You couldn't pay the rent in your former home.

WAM: My landlord was so pressing that I was obliged to pay him on the spot in order to avoid anything unpleasant, which caused me great embarrassment. But the fact is, I have done more work during my time here than in any other lodgings; and if it were not that I am plagued endlessly by gloomy thoughts which I can dispel only by force, I could do still more, for I live pleasantly, comfortably, and cheaply.

SP: But your debts have been building for some time, Wolfgang, and you went to your friend from the freemasons, Mr Pucher for help, which he gave. But it wasn't enough, and you feared for both your honour and your credit –

WAM: – the only two things I was anxious to preserve!

SP: So you set off on another tour of North East Europe, taking in Prague, Leipzig, Potsdam, and Berlin.

WAM: I did, yes. The Bohemians understand me.

SP: And you mentioned to me some requests you made to Constanze, whom you left behind. She was ill at the time.

WAM: A number of requests, yes.

SP: So what did you say?

WAM: Firstly, I beg you not to be melancholy. Second, that you will take care of yourself, and not expose yourself to the spring breeze. Third, that you will not go out and walk alone – indeed, it will be better not to walk at all. Fourth, that you will feel entirely assured of my love. I have not written you a single letter without placing your dear portrait before me.

SP: That's rather nice.

WAM: Fifth –

SP: – fifth? You clearly had a lot on your mind.

WAM: Fifth, I beg you not only to be careful of your honour and mine in your conduct, but to be equally guarded as to *appearances*.

SP: That sounds a bit like a reprimand, but I have heard she's fond of life's pleasures.

WAM: I said not to be angry at this request; indeed, it ought to make her love me all the better, after seeing the regard I have for my own honour.

SP: Possibly.

WAM: And sixthly, I wished she would give me more details in her letters.

SP: Ah, you wanted to know the Viennese gossip, news of what everyone was doing!

WAM: All these things interest me much. And remember, before going to bed every night, I conversed with her portrait for a good half hour, and the same when I awoke.

SP: You wrote very – er – loving letters home. How would it go?

WAM: 'Spruce up your sweet little nest, Constanze, because my little rascal here really deserves it; he has been very well-behaved but now he's itching to possess your –'

SP: – well, I think we're getting the gist.

WAM: And in one letter, I kissed her 1,095,060,437,082 times!

SP: That *is* a lot of kisses. You missed your wife.

WAM: I was as happy as a child at the thought of returning to her.

SP: And you couldn't say that about most of the relationships you had.

WAM: Yes, if people could see into my heart, I should almost feel ashamed.

SP: Why was that?

WAM: All there is cold, cold as ice. Were she with me, however, I would possibly take more pleasure in the kindnesses of those I met on tour, but really, all seemed to me so empty.

SP: And sadly, the tour did not make as much money as you hoped, and soon you were back to borrowing from Herr Puchberg again.

WAM: I would not have required so considerable a sum if I did not anticipate such heavy expenses to enable my wife to have the baths recommended for her – particularly as she had to go to Baden; though leeches relieved her sometimes.

SP: How did you approach Puchberg?

WAM: I said I would look upon him as my saviour on this side of the grave, for he'd enable me to enjoy good fortune hereafter on earth.

SP: So despite the success of your operas, you had a lot on your mind, with your money worries and Constanze's poor health.

WAM: I was indeed very unhappy, in alternate hope and fear.

SP: And of course you didn't like owing Puchberg so much.

WAM: Oh, if you could only know all the sorrow and care it caused me, but not being able to find any true friend, I was obliged then to get money from usurers.

SP: Money lenders?

WAM: Yes, but it took time to find the most Christian among that most unchristian race of men, which left me in a state of destitution.

SP: And the piano pupils, your bread and butter income – even they were dropping off.

WAM: I had two pupils but should really have liked eight. I asked Puchberg to let it be known that I did not object to giving lessons.

SP: Even though in your heart you didn't want to. And tell me, Wolfgang, did you make it harder for you, always running from Salzburg? You don't like the place I know, but at least it provides employment for five composers at any one time and maintains a small orchestra and choir, with the Catholic tradition encouraging both orchestras in church music and operatic style during service. Whilst running from it – well, it made you forever a foreigner, always a stranger.

WAM: Salzburg was no place for my talent. In the first place, professional musicians were not held in much consideration; and, secondly, one heard nothing. There is no theatre, no opera there; and if they really wished to have one, who is there to sing? For the last five or six years the Salzburg orchestra has always been rich in what is useless and unnecessary, but very poor in what is useful and indispensable.

SP: Your father found work there.

WAM: The thing that disgusts me with Salzburg – and I speak as I feel – is the impossibility of having any satisfactory relationship with the people; and that musicians are not in good repute there, and – well, that the Archbishop places no faith in the experience of intelligent persons who have seen the world!

SP: He prefers plodders.

WAM: If the Archbishop had only placed confidence in me, I could soon have made his music celebrated, of this there is no doubt. I was then pretty well-known – that is, the people all knew of me, even if I didn't know them.

SP: I understand.

WAM: The thing is, in Salzburg I never knew how I stood, I really didn't. At one time I was everything, at another, absolutely nothing. I neither desired so much nor so little, but still I wished to be something – if indeed I am something!

s p : Oh you are something, Wolfgang. And didn't Salieri say the same? He's sometimes accused of badmouthing you, but he loved *The Magic Flute*.

wa m : Oh yes, I called for Salieri and Cavalieri in the carriage, and took them to my box. You can't conceive how polite they both were, and how pleased not only with my music, but with the libretto and in short with everything.

s p : They saw a future for the work?

wa m : They said this was a work worthy of being performed at the greatest festivities, and before the greatest monarchs, and that they would certainly go very often to hear it.

s p : And Salieri? You know what people say.

wa m : Salieri both listened and looked attentively at everything, and from the symphony to the last chorus, there was not a single piece that did not call from him a 'Bravo!' It seemed they couldn't thank me enough for the pleasure I'd given them.

s p : And of course you also took your young son Carl to the opera.

wa m : Which gave him no small joy, yes.

s p : Because you felt there were some aspects of his education that were lacking. The school kept him physically fit but, well, that was about it.

WAM: The education there succeeds in producing a good peasant.

SP: What sort of a boy is he?

WAM: Carl is as he always is: as riotous as ever, chattering away as usual, yet even less willing to learn than before, because all he does at his school is run about the garden for five hours in the forenoon, and then the same after dinner.

SP: How do you know?

WAM: He told me so himself! In other words, the children do nothing but eat and drink, sleep and run about.

SP: It is so hard to find a decent school these days. But before we finish, tell me about Aloysia

WAM: Madame Lange?

SP: Well, Madame Lange as she now is. I heard her singing recently, and you were right all those years ago, she does have a fine voice. But how do you feel about her now? Your father, of course, thought you'd been a fool over her.

WAM: I was a fool about Madame Lange.

SP: That's very honest of you.

WAM: But what man is not when he's in love?

SP: True.

WAM: But I did truly love her and even now I feel she's not

indifferent towards me.

sp: Really?

wam: It is perhaps fortunate that her husband is a jealous booby, and never leaves her, so that I seldom have an opportunity of seeing her.

sp: A flame still burns?

wam: But in the meantime, I must withdraw 150 florins, for my landlord prefers the sound of gold to that of music.

sp: Which is a shame, Wolfgang – because if it were the other way round, your life would currently be much easier, would it not?

FIFTEEN

Heroes

I am always interested to find out whom people admire.

SP: Wolfgang, I want to ask you about your musical heroes. I've heard you criticize a few people. But whom out there do you admire?

WAM: Haydn knows better than any of us what will make an effect; when he chooses, he strikes like a thunderbolt; even if he's often prosy, after the manner of his time, there is always something in his music.

SP: I'm told you knew his masterpieces by heart.

WAM: Nobody can do everything – jest, terrify, cause laughter or move profoundly – like Joseph Haydn.

SP: And is this why you dedicated those quartets to him?

WAM: It was simply a duty I owed to him, as it was from him that I learned how to write quartets.

SP: And you've already spoken of your admiration for JS Bach, whom Baron Von Swieten introduced to you in 1782.

WAM: I went to his house every Sunday and nothing was played there but Bach and Handel. I made a collection of Bach's fugues.

SP: And you transcribed one of them – Bach's fugue No.5 in D major – and Baron von Swieten performed it as a quartet.

WAM: 'Well Mozart,' he said. 'You really have brought the old Johann Sebastian back to life! And for that, I give you my deepest thanks.'

SP: So I wasn't surprised when Thomas Attwood, your English pupil, told me that Bach's work, *The Well-Tempered Clavier*, was always lying open on your piano.

WAM: True.

SP: And then of course there was his son, Johann Christian, or the 'London Bach' as he was called – you were an admirer of his also, and you met each other in France?

WAM: Johann Christian Bach had been in Paris for a fortnight. He was to write a French opera, and was come only to hear the singers, whereupon he'd return to London, write the opera, and then come back to put it on the stage.

SP: But importantly, this wasn't your first meeting. Little Wolfgang had got to know him in London back in 1764, when apparently he took you on his knee and the two of you played on the harpsichord.

WAM: I remember!

SP: He was Music Master to the Queen, and I have an interesting report from Jahn on your relationship, which you might like to hear: 'He liked to play with the boy,' says Jahn. 'Bach took him upon his knee and went through a sonata with him, each in turn playing a measure with such precision that no one would have suspected two performers. He began a fugue, which Wolfgang took up and completed when Bach broke off.'

WAM: Yes, so you can easily imagine both his delight and mine when we met again. Perhaps his delight was not altogether sincere, but one must admit that he is an honorable man and does justice to all. I love him, as you know, with all my heart, and respect him. And this is what you can say about him: to my face and to others, he really praised me, not extravagantly, like some, but seriously and in earnest.

SP: Sometimes less is more.

WAM: And as an exercise I did a setting of the aria, *'Non so d'onde viene,'* * which he composed so beautifully. I did it because I know Bach so well, and the aria pleases me so much that I can't get it out of my head. I wanted to see whether or not, in spite of these things, I was able to make an aria that should not be a bit like Bach's. And it isn't a bit, not a bit like it.

SP: And finally, I believe you've spotted a hero for the future, because in 1787, a young man was in Vienna, improvising on a theme from *The Marriage of Figaro*. Ludwig van Beethoven was his name, I think.

WAM: Keep your eyes on him; he'll make the world talk of himself some day.

---

* *The lovely aria is No. 294 in Köchel's Catalog.*

SIXTEEN

Mozart's final bow

1791 was a busy year in terms of composition. Mozart started on his final opera The Clemency of Titus; *he was putting the finishing touches to* The Magic Flute *and working on the* Requiem — *a work commissioned by a Count for his dead wife, but which Mozart increasingly believed to be his own. He worked hard on this in his final months, composing late into the night, and even turning down requests for piano lessons. Apparently, much of it was written in the garden of Frau Von Trattner.*

His health was declining, however. He endured frequent fits of giddiness and nerves which were so unsettling that he had to remove his beloved pet canary when it was time to work.

sp: Music is your language.

wam: I cannot write poetically, for I am no poet.

sp: No.

wam: I cannot make fine artistic strokes that cast light and shadow, for I am no painter.

sp: Er...OK.

wam: I can neither by signs nor by pantomime express my thoughts and feelings, for I am no dancer; but I can by tones, for I am a musician.

sp: And a musician who has written many beautiful melodies, though not without a dissonance and darkness beneath the surface. Has death always haunted you?

WAM: I never lie down at night without thinking that young as I am, I may be no more before the next morning dawns.

SP: Your dear friend Hatzfeld died aged 31.

WAM: And I did not grieve for him, but deeply for myself, oh yes, and for all those who knew him as I did.

SP: And then there was Barisani, both your friend and your physician.

WAM: Another sudden death; I was so unfortunate to lose forever, in this world at least, that high-minded man, my dearest and best of friends, and the preserver of my life. For him, all was well, but for me, for us, it could never be – not until –

SP: Not until when?

WAM: Not until we are so blessed as to meet him again in a better world, and part no more.

SP: And in yourself, Wolfgang?

WAM: I can do nothing today but submit to doctors and apothecaries!

SP: A frightening thought. But – and how can I say this? – you cut a somewhat isolated figure in Vienna at present; there's a sense of sadness about you.

WAM: I can't describe what I have been feeling; a kind of

emptiness, yes, which hurts me dreadfully – a kind of longing which is never satisfied.

SP: Constanze thinks you should put aside your gloomy thoughts.

WAM: No, no! My feelings are too strong, and I sense I cannot last long.

SP: And yet here you are, working all the hours God sends on a requiem!

WAM: Did I not always say I was writing it for myself?

SP: You really think this is the end?

WAM: No doubt someone has given me poison.

SP: But who on earth would want to poison you?

WAM: I cannot get rid of this thought. God grant that some change may soon come to pass!

SP: Indeed.

WAM: And all will be well if we only have health; for happiness exists merely in the imagination –

These were Mozart's final words to me; for he left the room at this point, and we were never able to convene again. So, like the requiem he was working on at his death, our conversation was unfinished.

When I retuned to Vienna after some travel, I was stunned to

*discover that Wolfgang Amadeus Mozart, aged 35, was dead.
Whether it was a fever passing through the city at that time, or
some internal breakdown, no one is quite sure; though as weeks
became months, I wondered if it was not also a little to do with
exhaustion. During a creative life lasting 30 years – given that he
started composing when he was five – he produced a remarkable
24 operas, 19 Masses, 27 piano concertos, a further 24 concertos
for various instruments, over 60 symphonies, 23 string quartets,
36 violin sonatas, and 18 piano sonatas. Such endless work of the
mind is hard to imagine.*

*Concerning his death, Mozart may have been right to fear the
medical profession. In those final hours, the doctor was late on
the scene, and on arrival, ordered cold applications on Mozart's
burning head, which gave him such a shock that he never
regained consciousness. Towards midnight, Mozart started up, his
eyes fixed; his head then gently sank back, and he fell asleep. At
one o'clock in the morning, he was dead.*

* * *

*Apparently, Constanze refused to leave the body, laying herself on
top of it, hoping to catch the same illness. Mozart's small corpse
was clothed in the black garb of the Masonic brotherhood, and
laid out on a bier in his study by the piano – which, given its
owner, was surely one of the more fortunate keyboards down the
years.*

*I was glad to hear that in his final days, he had been cheered by
the success of* The Magic Flute. *He couldn't attend performances,
but put a clock by his bed, and imagined it, following the show in
spirit.*

He died almost penniless, of course, and in debt to his tailor, upholsterer, and many others. It is not for me to dwell on his inauspicious funeral and inelegant burial in a pauper's grave – so unmarked that Constanze never knew exactly where it was. But then this was not a marked death. Mozart's end was barely noticed by the public.

* * *

I pass on now only comments from those close to him at this time. It was Sophie, Constanze's sister, who was with him in his final hours, and to whom Mozart spoke these words:

WAM: 'Stay with me tonight. You must see me die. I have long had the taste of death on my tongue, I smell death, and who will stand by my Constanze, if you do not stay?'

And then there are his reported final words, spoken on his death bed:

WAM: 'And now I must go, just as it had become possible for me to live quietly. Now I must leave my art just as I had freed myself from the slavery of fashion, had broken the bonds of speculators, and won the privilege of following my own feelings and composing freely and independently whatever my heart prompted! I must away from my family, from my poor children in the moment when I should have been able better to care for their welfare!'

And in those days after his death, a number of things came to light, such as the notes he'd leave for Constanze. He'd sometimes go riding at 5:00am, and the ailing Constanze would wake to messages like this one:

WAM: 'Good morning, my darling wife! I hope that you

slept well, that you were undisturbed, that you will not rise too early, that you will not catch cold, nor stoop too much, nor overstrain yourself, nor scold your servants, nor stumble over the threshold of the adjoining room. Spare yourself all household worries till I come back. May no evil befall you. I'll be home at 8:00am punctually.'

There was professional praise. The contemporary composer, Carl Ditters von Dittersdorf, saw his abilities more clearly than some:

'Mozart leaves his listeners quite short of breath, for hardly has he prepared one beautiful idea, than another of even finer quality replaces the first, and so on until in the end, it is quite impossible to remember any one in particular.'

But I close with some words Constanze showed me on my last day in Vienna. They were from a letter he wrote to her during an enforced absence, and she cried as I read:

WAM: 'While writing the last page, my dearest, many a tear has fallen on it. But let us now be merry! Look! Swarms of kisses are flying about – quick! Catch some! I have caught three and how delicious they are!'

Afterword

The fame that might have given security to Mozart was impossible to establish in his lifetime. Most of his compositions were only heard in the place where he happened to be at the time, and not many were published. By contemporary standards, they were considered difficult to play and hard to understand. Emperor Joseph II *called his* Don Giovanni *'too meaty'; and believed* The Marriage of Figaro *had 'too many notes in it'. The Emperor was no great music critic, but perhaps spoke for his age.*

For a musical career these days, the first task is to find a secure job and a patron. Leipzig City Council had supported JS Bach, and the Princes Esterházy supported Haydn; but no one offered such support to Mozart.

It's time to close. But I mention this: as I travelled back from Vienna, I shared a carriage with Mark Warmanus, the famous impresario. He had heard much Mozart on his travels, and I record our conversation:

M W: I believe all honest musicians concur that he was indeed a genius, Simon, with a seat at the very top composers' table.

S P: Really?

M W: He was also, of course, a phenomenal performer, gifted critic, and had a quite astonishing musical memory. A conduit for the most perfectly shaped musical argument, exquisitely proportioned phrases, deep understanding of drama and emotion, sublime harmonies, he wrote for almost every secular and sacred musical group of players and singers that existed, sonatas and concerti for nearly every solo instrument

– including the newly invented clarinet.

SP: Could he do it all?

MW: He could indeed do it all, Simon; Wolfgang could do it all.

The end

Paperbacks also available from White Crow Books

Marcus Aurelius—*Meditations*
ISBN 978-1-907355-20-2

Elsa Barker—*Letters from a Living Dead Man*
ISBN 978-1-907355-83-7

Elsa Barker—*War Letters from the Living Dead Man*
ISBN 978-1-907355-85-1

Elsa Barker—*Last Letters from the Living Dead Man*
ISBN 978-1-907355-87-5

Richard Maurice Bucke—*Cosmic Consciousness*
ISBN 978-1-907355-10-3

G. K. Chesterton—*The Everlasting Man*
ISBN 978-1-907355-03-5

G. K. Chesterton—*Heretics*
ISBN 978-1-907355-02-8

G. K. Chesterton—*Orthodoxy*
ISBN 978-1-907355-01-1

Arthur Conan Doyle—*The Edge of the Unknown*
ISBN 978-1-907355-14-1

Arthur Conan Doyle—*The New Revelation*
ISBN 978-1-907355-12-7

Arthur Conan Doyle—*The Vital Message*
ISBN 978-1-907355-13-4

Arthur Conan Doyle with Simon Parke—*Conversations with Arthur Conan Doyle*
ISBN 978-1-907355-80-6

Leon Denis with Arthur Conan Doyle—*The Mystery of Joan of Arc*
ISBN 978-1-907355-17-2

The Earl of Dunraven—*Experiences in Spiritualism with D. D. Home*
ISBN 978-1-907355-93-6

Meister Eckhart with Simon Parke—*Conversations with Meister Eckhart*
ISBN 978-1-907355-18-9

Kahlil Gibran—*The Forerunner*
ISBN 978-1-907355-06-6

Kahlil Gibran—*The Madman*
ISBN 978-1-907355-05-9

Kahlil Gibran—*The Prophet*
ISBN 978-1-907355-04-2

Kahlil Gibran—*Sand and Foam*
ISBN 978-1-907355-07-3

Kahlil Gibran—*Jesus the Son of Man*
ISBN 978-1-907355-08-0

Kahlil Gibran—*Spiritual World*
ISBN 978-1-907355-09-7

Hermann Hesse—*Siddhartha*
ISBN 978-1-907355-31-8

D. D. Home—*Incidents in my Life Part 1*
ISBN 978-1-907355-15-8

Mme. Dunglas Home; edited, with an Introduction, by Sir Arthur Conan Doyle—*D. D. Home: His Life and Mission*
ISBN 978-1-907355-16-5

Edward C. Randall—*Frontiers of the Afterlife*
ISBN 978-1-907355-30-1

Lucius Annaeus Seneca—*On Benefits*
ISBN 978-1-907355-19-6

Rebecca Ruter Springer—*Intra Muros—My Dream of Heaven*
ISBN 978-1-907355-11-0

W. T. Stead—*After Death or Letters from Julia: A Personal Narrative*
ISBN 978-1-907355-89-9

Leo Tolstoy, edited by Simon Parke—*Forbidden Words*
ISBN 978-1-907355-00-4

Leo Tolstoy—*A Confession*
ISBN 978-1-907355-24-0

Leo Tolstoy—*The Gospel in Brief*
ISBN 978-1-907355-22-6

Leo Tolstoy—*The Kingdom of God is Within You*
ISBN 978-1-907355-27-1

Leo Tolstoy—*My Religion: What I Believe*
ISBN 978-1-907355-23-3

Leo Tolstoy—*On Life*
ISBN 978-1-907355-91-2

Leo Tolstoy—*Twenty-three Tales*
ISBN 978-1-907355-29-5

Leo Tolstoy—*What is Religion and other writings*
ISBN 978-1-907355-28-8

Leo Tolstoy—*Work While Ye Have the Light*
ISBN 978-1-907355-26-4

Leo Tolstoy with Simon Parke—*Conversations with Tolstoy*
ISBN 978-1-907355-25-7

Vincent Van Gogh with Simon Parke—*Conversations with Van Gogh*
ISBN 978-1-907355-95-0

Howard Williams with an Introduction by Leo Tolstoy—*The Ethics of Diet: An Anthology of Vegetarian Thought*
ISBN 978-1-907355-21-9

Allan Kardec—*The Spirits Book*
ISBN 978-1-907355-98-1

Wolfgang Amadeus Mozart with Simon Parke—*Conversations with Mozart*
ISBN 978-1-907661-38-9

Jesus of Nazareth with Simon Parke—*Conversations with Jesus of Nazareth*
ISBN 978-1-907661-41-9

Rudolf Steiner—*Christianity as a Mystical Fact: And the Mysteries of Antiquity*
ISBN 978-1-907661-52-5

Thomas à Kempis with Simon Parke—*The Imitation of Christ*
ISBN 978-1-907661-58-7

Emanuel Swedenborg—*Heaven and Hell*
ISBN 978-1-907661-55-6

P.D. Ouspensky—*Tertium Organum: The Third Canon of Thought*
ISBN 978-1-907661-47-1

Dwight Goddard—*The Buddhist Bible*
ISBN 978-1-907661-44-0

Leo Tolstoy—*The Death of Ivan Ilyich*
ISBN 978-1-907661-10-5

Leo Tolstoy—*Resurrection*
ISBN 978-1-907661-09-9

All titles available as eBooks, and selected titles available in Hardback and Audiobook formats from www.whitecrowbooks.com

www.ingramcontent.com/pod-product-compliance
Lightning Source LLC
LaVergne TN
LVHW011201080426
835508LV00007B/541